The Boo

A Guide to Understanding

The Book of Revelation:
A Guide to Understanding

Raymond E. Parry

Illustrations by Pegi Ballenger

RIDGEWOOD PUBLISHING

DEDICATION

This book is dedicated to my professors at Bethel Theological Seminary who taught me how to interpret scripture, to my adult classes at First Presbyterian Church of Colorado Springs, CO and Cross of Christ Community Church of Lakeville, MN who joined me in studying this often confusing and sometimes disturbing revelation, and to my wife Pegi, who not only contributed the illustrations, but patiently listened to and commented on every chapter as it was being prepared and presented.

Table of Contents

Index to Illustrations

INTRODUCTION

Welcome to our study of the Revelation of St. John the Divine, as it is entitled in the King James version. Revelation is a book of mystery to many people because of the wild imagery John used to comfort and encourage Christians in the first century. John tells us he was in exile on the island of Patmos when he wrote this book. Scholars have debated whether this imprisonment occurred while Nero was emperor of Rome from 54 to 68 AD and before the fall of Jerusalem in 70 AD, or when Domitian was emperor from 81-96 AD. The weight of the testimony of the church fathers leads nearly all scholars to conclude that Domitian was the emperor under whom John was imprisoned around 94-95 AD. The Emperor Domitian had demanded that people address him as, "My Lord and God," or face the consequences. Christians were hauled before local judges and required to worship Domitian recanting their faith in Christ. If they refused, the punishment was death or imprisonment. In John's case the punishment was exile to the prison colony on Patmos as an old man. He was the last of the original 12 apostles of Jesus, the son of Zebedee the fisherman. John probably expected to end his days in some lonely anonymous grave on Patmos. Instead he was released when emperor Nerva came to the throne in 96 AD, and John returned to Ephesus where he continued his ministry, writing his Gospel at the urging of other church leaders before he finally died at an advanced age. While John was on Patmos, he had a series of visions that he wrote down and sent to seven of the churches of Western Turkey. To each church, he reported a message from the heavenly Jesus whom he saw in his vision recorded in Revelation chapter 1.

The short letters to these churches can be found in Revelation chapters 2 and 3. All seven of these letters are pointed directly at the Christians in the churches of Western Turkey, known as Asia in those days, but they're also pointed directly at us. The problems they faced are very similar to the problems we face today. The temptations they faced are very similar to the temptations we face today. To those Christians facing persecution like those in Ephesus, Smyrna and Philadelphia, their letters offer the comfort of a powerful Christ who will win over evil, and bring Christians home to be with Him. To those Christians who have compromised their faith with popular religions such as those more worldly Christians in Pergamum and Thyatira, their letters call for repentance and offer the comfort of forgiveness with the strength to stand true. And finally, to those who trust in their own strength and abilities like some Christians at Sardis and Laodicea, the patient Christ summons them to return to His care. To all who overcome the pressures and temptations to turn their backs on their faith and leave the Kingdom of God, Christ holds out the promise of an eternal life of fellowship with him and the Father and all the saints and angels in heaven. The message was not much different than John had heard from Jesus' lips decades before. What was new was an expanded account in vivid imagery of what would happen when Jesus returns to finalize the Kingdom of which all believers in Him are members.

Mark tells us in his gospel, chapter 1, verse 14, that when Jesus began to preach, He proclaimed the good news of God by saying, "the time is at hand, the kingdom of God is near. Repent and believe the good news." In the Sermon on the Mount in Matthew's gospel, Jesus tells us how to live as members of this Kingdom of God. The Kingdom of God is an important theme of Jesus' teachings. But the book of Revelation is also about the Kingdom of God. It's a message to believers throughout the ages that no matter how hard life gets, no matter how badly you are persecuted for your faith, God is alive and in charge and active, and He will win over the evil that we see in our world. If you keep that central theme in mind as you study the book of Revelation, you'll have a better understanding of the encouraging message John is trying to pass on to Christians living in tumultuous times.

As you begin this study, it would be helpful to have an open Bible and follow along as we turn to not just Revelation, but also the Old Testament prophets and Paul's letters to help us in our understanding of John's images and visions. Readings from the World English Bible have been included, but it often helps in understanding to refer to other versions.

Several chapters have study questions at their end for use in small group studies, or to help clarify and broaden the thrust of the commentary.

At the end of this study, you will find a list of commentaries and thematic studies that you may want to consult from a library or obtain from online bookstores that will go into more detail in various areas that spark your curiosity.

In the Appendix you'll also find a list of all the scripture references, a glossary of selected names and keywords, and definitions for Greek and Hebrew words.

1

JOHN'S VISION OF THE HEAVENLY JESUS

The first question we have to answer is: What does the word "revelation" mean? The book of Revelation belongs to a class of literature known as apocalyptic, which literally means "uncovering something that was hidden", which we could shorten to "revealing" from which we get "Revelation." In Greek, the language in which this book was written, the first word simply says *apokolupsis* which told the early Greek-speaking Christians that what followed would be filled with images, analogies, and allegories. Things written here might not mean literally what the words say, as they would in a gospel like Matthew's, or a letter like Paul's to the Romans, nor is it poetry like Psalms. Instead, here they were going to discover secrets from God about what He is doing in the world, and they knew it would be filled with unusual images and figures of animals that would stand for people and nations and movements in history. They knew it because they had seen this kind of literature before. Much of the book of Daniel is apocalyptic, and there were other books circulating in both Jewish and Christian circles that were apocalyptic as well, such as the Book of Enoch. They knew how to interpret these kinds of books and gain comfort and insight from them, knowing that the meaning would stay hidden from non-believers, who couldn't make sense of the wild images. Unfortunately, because of the nearly two thousand years that separates us from the early Christians, some of the meanings of Revelation are hidden from us as well. But because hope in the future is such an important part of the Christian faith, we shouldn't relegate the book of Revelation to a dusty part of our library, but should try to understand it and what it means to our lives today.

But before we get into reading the hidden meanings in Revelation, we've got to ask, who is John? There have been several proposals over the centuries as to who this John was. The earliest and simplest proposal was that this particular John was John the son of Zebedee, one of Jesus' disciples. That's the witness of the early church fathers Irenaeus and Justin, who lived in the middle of the second century. They tell us that John was exiled to the island of Patmos during the persecution of the emperor Domitian, and it was there that John wrote the Revelation. Later on, other commentators noticed that the Greek used in Revelation was very rough and crude, while the gospel of John is very simple and smooth, so they suggested the two books were written by different people. And at least one scholar went so far as to suggest that Revelation was written by John the Baptist, because its dramatic style would fit him better than it would a supposedly meek and mild John the apostle. Of course, as you may remember, John the son of Zebedee had a nickname, Boanerges, which meant "son of Thunder," so I suspect he was quite capable of writing a book like Revelation. I think the differences between the Gospel of John and Revelation can be easily explained by assuming John used an educated secretary to help him when he was writing his Gospel as a very old man, but while in Exile on Patmos, he didn't have a secretary and had to write it himself, and he wrote as a fisherman, not as a scholar. I have no trouble assigning this book to John the son of Zebedee, who was one of Jesus' earliest followers. Now an old man in exile, having had a lifetime to think about the meaning of the life, death and resurrection of his friend and master, Jesus, he wants to pass along the assurance that God is in control. No matter what problems come our way because we've chosen to follow Jesus just as John did so long ago, we are on the right road. This is the way that leads to life.

Since verse 1 starts off with the announcement of a revelation, let's look at John's opening words to learn more.

REVELATION 1:1-3

1 "This is the Revelation of Jesus Christ, which God gave him to show to his servants the things which must happen soon, which he sent and made known by his angel to his servant, John, 2 who testified to God's word, and of the testimony of Jesus Christ, about everything that he saw. 3 Blessed is he who reads and those who hear the words of the prophecy, and keep the things that are written in it, for the time is at hand."

Well, what was this revelation to John about? The next words in verse 1 are "of Jesus Christ." In Greek, that could be taken two different ways. It could mean that this book contains "the revelation about Jesus Christ," or it could mean "the revelation from Jesus Christ." In some ways both are true. One of the main characters in this book is Jesus Christ, but I think the emphasis is that this revelation comes from Jesus to us through John, so that we will know what's really going on in this world, rather than what we might think is going on from our limited understanding. Verse 1 goes on to say, "which God gave to Him to show to His servants" — and that's us and all the

Christians who have come before us, and who may come after us. Jesus is going to show his servants "what must soon happen." Literally, the Greek says, "what is necessary to happen quickly or suddenly." You could take that as meaning what's written here is going to be happening any day, or any minute now; or you could take it as meaning there won't be any warning — this is going to be a surprise that will catch many people off guard. What we read in Revelation is going to be a surprise to those who haven't read it, or aren't interested at all in obeying God, or who don't believe that God is in control, or don't think there's any need for God in our modern secular culture. While there may be things here that we have difficulty understanding today, those early Christians who heard this book read to them in church gatherings could grasp what it meant. They heard that no matter how violent and horrible the persecutions they were suffering might be, God was going to turn the tables on the oppressors, and evil would be destroyed along with all the servants of that evil power. It's almost like going to a James Bond movie: you know that the hero is going to win and that all the bad guys are going to meet their doom.

To try and understand why the early Christians were so certain that the end of the world was coming soon, and that God was going to march in and destroy the Romans as well as the unbelieving Jews and Gentiles, try to put yourself in their place. On Good Friday, Jesus the Messiah had been put to death on the cross. His followers had expected Jesus, as God's Messiah, to take over and rule the country as a new King David, but instead Jesus had died at the hands of the ruthless Roman procurator, Pontius Pilate. They were shocked, they were disappointed, they were angry, and they were afraid. Would they be next? Was there any place they could hide that the Roman army couldn't find them? But then, on Easter, Jesus rose from the dead, and his disciples celebrated. Jesus was alive! God had triumphed. And when Jesus left them again and rose into the heavens, they thought he would certainly return in judgment at the head of God's army. It would happen any day: the heavens would open, the skies would be filled with angels on chariots of fire, coming with swords and spears to wipe out all the evil-doers.

You can see that expectation throughout the books that make up our New Testament. In Paul's first letter to the Thessalonians, which was probably the first letter he wrote to one of his churches in Greece, he encourages the young Christians by saying that Christ will come again with angels and the dead will rise from the grave, and we'll all be with the Lord forever.

16 "For the Lord himself will descend from heaven with a shout, with the voice of the archangel, and with God's trumpet. The dead in Christ will rise first, 17 then we who are alive, who are left, will be caught up together with them in the clouds, to meet the Lord in the air. So we will be with the Lord forever. 18 Therefore comfort one another with these words." (I Thessalonians 4:16-18)

Apparently, some believers among the Thessalonians took that to mean they should rid themselves of all their earthly cares, quit their jobs, sell their possessions, and go to the mountaintop to wait for the Lord. But, expecting the Lord to return doesn't mean we should sit around and wait. Paul goes on to say in I Thessalonians that we don't know the dates or times when Jesus will come again, so stop worrying about it!

1 "But concerning the times and the seasons, brothers, you have no need that anything be written to you. 2 For you yourselves know well that the day of the Lord comes like a thief in the night." (I Thessalonians 5:1-2)

Paul says in the meantime, keep on working, keep on living, keep on witnessing to others about Christ. All we need to know is that Jesus will come again, and he will come suddenly, "like a thief in the night," with no warning. The apostle James wrote to Jewish Christians in Jerusalem and those dispersed throughout the Empire that believers needed to be patient like a farmer who has to wait for his crops to grow.

> 7 *"Be patient therefore, brothers, until the coming of the Lord. Behold, the farmer waits for the precious fruit of the earth, being patient over it, until it receives the early and late rain. 8 You also be patient. Establish your hearts, for the coming of the Lord is at hand." (James 5:7-8)*

The Lord is coming, as sure as seeds sprout and grow into grain, but until He comes, be patient and stand firm in the faith. In Mark's gospel, which was written for the Roman churches, we read that Jesus talked about His coming again.

> 26 *"Then they will see the Son of Man coming in clouds with great power and glory. 27 Then he will send out his angels, and will gather together his chosen ones from the four winds, from the ends of the earth to the ends of the sky." (Mark 13:26-27)*

This is His assurance to us that He will come again. But then He says even He doesn't know when that will be.

> 32 *"But of that day or that hour no one knows, not even the angels in heaven, nor the Son, but only the Father. 33*

Watch, keep alert, and pray; for you don't know when the time is. 34 "It is like a man, traveling to another country, having left his house, and given authority to his servants, and to each one his work, and also commanded the doorkeeper to keep watch. 35 Watch therefore, for you don't know when the lord of the house is coming, whether at evening, or at midnight, or when the rooster crows, or in the morning; 36 lest coming suddenly he might find you sleeping. 37 What I tell you, I tell all: Watch." (Mark 13:32-37)

After telling us He's coming again, He says that no one knows the day or hour: He doesn't know, the angels don't know, only God knows. Jesus gives the example in verses 34-37 of a home owner who goes away on a trip and leaves his servants in charge. They don't know when he'll be back, but they keep watch, and keep to their duties, because they want to be ready if he comes back suddenly.

So throughout all the regions and every nationality that made up the early church — Greece (Thessalonians), Jerusalem (James), and Rome (Mark) — we read the same story: Christ is coming again, but we don't know when, so keep on living, but live expectantly with hope. The book of Revelation reinforced that hope by saying in effect, "it may get hard, but God's going to win."

Look back at the rest of verse 1 of Revelation, "He made it known by sending his angel to his servant John." The words "made known" translate the Greek verb "signing." So literally, the Greek says, "and he showed it (what must come soon) in signs by sending a message through his angel to his servant John." John tells us right up front that what we're about to read comes to us in signs. It's almost like John's telling us to pay careful attention because in effect God has gone along the highway of life planting Burma Shave signs down the road side. Although you can read each sign, you can't make sense out of the message until you've read the whole thing.

Verse 2 continues by telling us what John did with this message from the angel. It reads, "who testified to the word of God and the testimony of Jesus Christ: everything he saw." John saw these things as visions given to him by God, not as dreams or nightmares. Many of these visions seem like abstract paintings, like a Chagall, a Picasso, or a Dali; they may portray a reality, but not in the same literal style as Rembrandt or DaVinci. The visions John relates to us should not just be read: they have to be seen with the imagination.

This section closes with a benediction: verse 3 says we are blessed if we read the words of this prophecy, we are blessed if we hear it, and we are blessed if we take it to heart. Verse 3 uses the word "prophecy," but to understand what prophecy is all about, we've got to look at the Old Testament. In the Old Testament, prophets are not so much seers of the future as spokesmen for God. They spoke the word of God to the people of God about current situations, and they basically said, "If things don't change around here, bad things are going to happen to you." Invariably, the people ignored the warnings, and bad things did happen. When the people didn't stop worshipping other gods and abused the poor and needy, kings and armies would sweep in and destroy cities and carry the Jewish people off into captivity. But, there was another side of prophecy spoken to those captive Jews, saying "Trust God and things will get better."

The book of Revelation is more than just apocalyptic, because it contains that emphasis of prophecy: there are warnings to those who choose to ignore God, and blessings to those who follow their Savior. The blessings of God come to those who do more than read it, and do more than hear it. They come to those who take to heart that the time is near. This book is an encouragement, then, to have hope, to know that God is in control, and that the solution to the problems of this world is coming soon, even if we don't know exactly when.

Let's look at John's opening words to the seven churches in Asia in Revelation 1:4-8.

REVELATION 1:4-8

4 *"John, to the seven assemblies that are in Asia: Grace to you and peace, from God, who is and who was and who is to come; and from the seven Spirits who are before his throne; 5 and from Jesus Christ, the faithful witness, the firstborn of the dead, and the ruler of the kings of the earth. To him who loves us, and washed us from our sins by his blood; 6 and he made us to be a Kingdom, priests to his God and Father; to him be the glory and the dominion forever and ever. Amen. 7 Behold, he is coming with the clouds, and every eye will see him, including those who pierced him. All the tribes of the earth will mourn over him. Even so, Amen. 8 "I am the Alpha and the Omega," says the Lord God, "who is and who was and who is to come, the Almighty.""*

In verse 4, the word translated "assemblies" is *ekklesia* which means literally "called-out ones" and is usually translated in English as "churches." When we see the word "church" we frequently think of a building of brick, stone, or wood with a steeple rising to the sky. But in the first century, Christians gathered in homes or borrowed meeting places for worship and fellowship. The book of Revelation is in the form of a letter to these assemblies of believers (or churches). Specifically, it's a letter from John to the seven churches in the province of Asia. These seven churches are named in verse 11 and all these are cities in western Turkey. Now, there were more than seven churches in this region, the church at Colossae, for example. So, why were only these seven named? Some commentators say these seven cities were the regional mail centers for the Roman province of Asia, and that letters going to churches in each of these cities would be re-copied and sent out to other churches connected to each of these cities like spokes on a wheel. Others point out that each city was a day's ride on a circular route that began and ended at Ephesus, as you can see from this map.

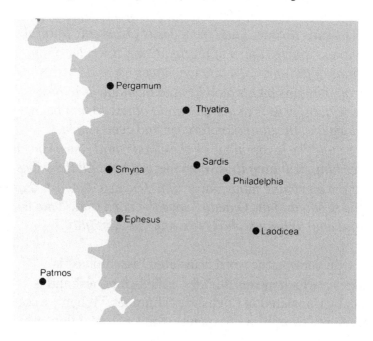

But there is another way to look at it. The number seven is a special number to John. He uses it sixty-three times in Revelation. In chapter 1, we see seven churches, seven spirits, seven lamp stands, seven stars, and further on we'll read about seven angels, seven seals, seven trumpets and seven bowls. In the Bible, seven is a number that indicates completeness, just like there are seven days in a week. To talk about or cover a subject fully and completely, it helps to take it from seven different perspectives or angles. So, seven churches could be a way of saying all churches, or the whole church, of which these seven are prime examples.

In the same way, look at "seven spirits before the throne" that you find in verse 4. You may see in a footnote an alternate translation, "the seven-fold Spirit." Many commentators see the seven spirits or the seven-fold Spirit referring back to Isaiah 11:1-2.

> *1 "A shoot will come out of the stock of Jesse,*
> *and a branch out of his roots will bear fruit.*
> *2 Yahweh's Spirit will rest on him:*
> *the spirit of wisdom and understanding,*
> *the spirit of counsel and might,*
> *the spirit of knowledge and of the fear of*
> *Yahweh." (Isaiah 11:1-2)*

The Septuagint, which is the Greek translation of the Hebrew Old Testament done in Alexandria around 250 BC, inserts one more spirit, godliness, making seven inspiring characteristics of the Spirit of God. Verse 1 of the Isaiah passage was seen in the early church as a prophecy about Jesus being the Messiah, the long awaited son of King David. In verse 2, we find the Holy Spirit of God coming on him and infusing him with all the characteristics of greatness: the Spirit of the Lord rests on him, which means it's a permanent part of his being; the spirit gives him wisdom, understanding, counsel, power, knowledge, godliness and fear of the Lord. Altogether, the Holy Spirit is seen from seven perspectives, inspiring seven godly characteristics of the person of God. In the Talmud, Sanhedrin 93b, this verse is linked directly to the Messiah.

> "The Messiah — as it is written, And the spirit of the Lord shall rest upon him, the spirit of wisdom and understanding, the spirit of counsel and might, the spirit of knowledge of the fear of the Lord." (Talmud, Sanhedrin 93b)

We're going to find throughout Revelation that the images John gives us are based on pictures we'll find in the Old Testament, particularly from the prophecies of Daniel, Zechariah, and Isaiah. It's an important principle in studying the New Testament that you must refer back to the Old Testament. Remember, for the early readers of the books of the New Testament as they were being written, circulated and read, that the only Bible they had was the Old Testament. It was natural for John to expect his readers to be familiar with all these images out of the Old Testament and to use those familiar images to interpret what God has been doing, is doing, and will do in their lives. So, in Revelation, Jewish Christians in particular would have recognized John's use of Isaiah 11:2 in Revelation 1:4 when he reminded them of the seven-fold completeness of the Spirit in their lives.

Note that in Revelation 1:4-5 we discover a picture of the Trinity. In just two verses, John describes the members of the Trinity: Father, Holy Spirit (the seven-fold Spirit), and Son. In verse 4, John starts his letter with a blessing.

He says, "Grace and peace to you from the One who is and the One who was, and the One who is to come." That phrase "the One who is and the One who was and the One who is to come" is a title belonging to God the Father. Jewish people of the first century frequently used the Greek words *ho own*, which literally means, "the one who is" or "the One," as a replacement for God's Holy Name. Remember when Moses asked God what His name was in Exodus 3:14? God replied, "I AM WHO I AM." There's no sense of time in that statement—it's valid for all time. You'll also find the same phrase "the One who is, the One who was and the One who is to come" repeated in verse 8, which finishes this section, where God describes Himself. John is reminding us of God's eternity, spanning all time: past, present, and future. God sees what's happening to us now, how He's prepared us for it in the past, and He knows what will happen to us in the future. The whole concept of time in the Bible is that of a continuum, a straight line of days, years, and centuries. Time runs from the distant past at the moment of creation that we find in the book of Genesis, to the distant future of the destruction of evil, and then the re-creation of a new world by God at the end of the book of Revelation.

For human beings, time runs straight on, and we continually get older and older from the moment we're born until the moment we die. There are no cycles of history in the Bible, no reincarnation where we return to do it again until we get it right. But for God, since He created this world, time has no relevance. To Him, past, present, and future are all the same; they all exist at the same time, if you will. God could see you being born from the moment He created the world. He knew what would happen to you even when Abraham, Isaac, and Jacob walked this earth. He knew you would come to faith in

Him. He knew what struggles you would have in life. He gave you the opportunities to grow and build character, so that you could handle those struggles. The Psalmist says:

> *15 "My frame wasn't hidden from you,*
> *when I was made in secret,*
> *woven together in the depths of the earth.*
> *16 Your eyes saw my body.*
> *In your book they were all written,*
> *the days that were ordained for me,*
> *when as yet there were none of them." (Psalm 139:15-16)*

God also knew when you would die, and under what circumstances. And He knew whether you would be with Him for eternity, or whether you would choose to be separated from Him for eternity. For human beings, eternity stretches out before us in a line so long we can't see the end of it. It's very hard for us to grasp. But for God, eternity is NOW. When the Bible says we have eternal life when we accept Jesus as Savior, it means we immediately enter God's eternity. We don't have to wait until we die to know that we are with God — eternal life begins now.

We discussed earlier how the seven spirits or seven-fold Spirit mentioned in verse 4 refers to Isaiah 11:2 and encompasses the work of the Holy Spirit, the second member of the Trinity. In verse 5, John goes on to include the third member of the Trinity, Jesus. John calls Jesus the faithful witness, the firstborn from the dead, and the ruler of the kings of the earth. The Greek word for witness is *martus* or martyr. When we think of the word martyr, we think of someone who dies for what they believe. But what it really means is someone who witnesses to something. We already encountered this word martyr in verse 2. When John says he testifies to what he saw, and to the testimony of Jesus Christ, the words "testify" and "testimony" also come from the word martyr. John says, not only is he a witness to what he saw, but Jesus is the ultimate witness to the existence, the compassion, and the power of God. By living among us as God would live, and loving us as God would love, Jesus showed us what God is like, because we are forgetful people. We may know in our heads all the truths about God, but when the hard times come, and we're sick, or hurt, or feeling incredible pressure, it's not our heads that control our feelings and behavior. We're anxious and afraid, and it's those inner child-like fears that are in control. That's why knowing what's in all the books in the Bible, or believing all the doctrines of the church, isn't enough to get you through life: you've got to have that personal faith relationship with Jesus Christ that brings eternal life.

Jesus witnessed to the ultimate power of God by his resurrection. Death doesn't have power over God, or those who believe in Him. The kings and rulers of the earth may think they have that ultimate power; they may think they can order armies here and there; can even push the button and destroy everything in a nuclear holocaust. But while they are busy extending their power, God plants a tiny seed of faith that grows up to destroy them and crush their empires, just like He sent Jesus as a tiny baby to crush the power of evil in our world. When they tried to kill Him, Jesus became a witness that God has power even over death itself. When the early Christians were seized and put in the arenas to be killed by lions, the early rulers may have thought they were ending a threat to their power. But it didn't work. Those rulers are gone, their kingdoms are gone, but the Christian faith is still going strong, because Jesus is ruler even over them.

John goes on to tell us three things in verses 5 and 6 that apply not only to those early Christians being persecuted for their faith, but also to us in our lives today. We are loved, we are freed from our sins by his blood, and we are members and priests of God's Kingdom. God loves us, so what do we care if the world doesn't love us as long as God loves us? We have been freed from our sins, so why should we listen to those inner voices that accuse us of still being guilty? We are members of God's Kingdom, in fact, we <u>are</u> God's Kingdom because his spirit is within us, so what power do earthly governments that claim to have power over us really have over us? The answer is none.

Verse 7 is taken partly from a vision the prophet Daniel experienced.

13 "I saw in the night visions, and behold, there came with the clouds of the sky one like a son of man, and he came even to the ancient of days, and they brought him near before him. 14 Dominion was given him, and glory, and a kingdom, that all the peoples, nations, and languages should serve him. His dominion is an everlasting dominion, which will not pass away, and his kingdom that which will not be destroyed." (Daniel 7:13-14)

In Daniel we read that the Son of Man has power given to Him by God who is called the Ancient of Days, to rule over all the earth forever. You cannot destroy His kingdom — it will last forever. Do not fear, John says, Jesus the Messiah is coming just as it was promised. And then in Zechariah 12:10, which is quoted in the second half of Revelation 1:7, we read that the Jews will finally grieve for rejecting God's Messiah who came to save them.

¹⁰ *"I will pour on David's house, and on the inhabitants of Jerusalem, the spirit of grace and of supplication; and they will look to me whom they have pierced; and they shall mourn for him, as one mourns for his only son, and will grieve bitterly for him, as one grieves for his firstborn." (Zechariah 12:10)*

In Revelation 1:7, John extends that to all the peoples of the earth. When Jesus comes again, everyone will mourn that they did not respond to God's call, that they persecuted God's Messiah and God's people. John says this to comfort Christians who were feeling that the whole world was against them. When they stood for righteousness and truth, for morality, for honoring marriage, for peace and brotherhood, they were persecuted as haters of the human race. Their words were twisted to make good sound like evil, while the opposing evils were twisted to make them sound good.

John concludes verse 7 by saying, "So shall it be!" or "Amen." The word translated "So shall it be" is actually the one Greek word, *nai*, which simply means "Yes!" It's an exclamation, an agreement with the prophecies. It's like saying "Go for it, God," "Do it!" the same meaning as "Amen" in Hebrew. John closes out his introduction by reporting what God says in verse 8, "I am the Alpha and the Omega," which are the first and last letters of the Greek alphabet. God is the beginning and the end. God pronounced the first word in Genesis that created our world, and He will have the last word in Revelation that recreates our world. The last word in this section, "Almighty" is the Greek word *pantokratōr*, the Greek equivalent of the Hebrew word *Tsabaot*, meaning "Lord of the Hosts of Heaven." Heaven is conceived of as a place filled with armies of angels at God's beck and call; angels who not only watch out for believers in God during their days on earth, but will come to destroy those who do not believe during the last days as proclaimed by the prophets. Not only is God the beginning and end of all creation, and the one totally unlimited by time, the One who is, who was, and the One who will come, but He is also the Almighty, the Lord of all the hosts of heaven.

This was a strong message of comfort to the early Christians who were being arrested and brought before the magistrates on charges of just being Christians. But it is the same today. It is not easy to live the Christian life that Jesus taught us to live in the Sermon on the Mount. There are plenty of challenges every day of our lives to morality, to honesty, and to integrity. By and large, the world would prefer not to be burdened by Christians, who get in the way of a pragmatic and opportunistic way of life. But the message of Revelation is to hang in there. God is behind you, and God will win.

In the next section of Revelation chapter 1, John explains how his first vision came about and what it was like to see Jesus glorified.

REVELATION 1:9-20

9 *"I John, your brother and partner with you in the oppression, Kingdom, and perseverance in Christ Jesus, was on the isle that is called Patmos because of God's Word and the testimony of Jesus Christ.* 10 *I was in the Spirit on the Lord's day, and I heard behind me a loud voice, like a trumpet* 11 *saying, "What you see, write in a book and send to the seven assemblies: to Ephesus, Smyrna, Pergamum, Thyatira, Sardis, Philadelphia, and to Laodicea."* 12 *I turned to see the voice that spoke with me. Having turned, I saw seven golden lamp stands.*

¹³ And among the lamp stands was one like a son of man, clothed with a robe reaching down to his feet, and with a golden sash around his chest. ¹⁴ His head and his hair were white as white wool, like snow. His eyes were like a flame of fire. ¹⁵ His feet were like burnished brass, as if it had been refined in a furnace. His voice was like the voice of many waters. ¹⁶ He had seven stars in his right hand. Out of his mouth proceeded a sharp two-edged sword. His face was like the sun shining at its brightest. ¹⁷ When I saw him, I fell at his feet like a dead man. He laid his right hand on me, saying, "Don't be afraid. I am the first and the last, ¹⁸ and the Living one. I was dead, and behold, I am alive forever and ever. Amen. I have the keys of Death and of Hades. ¹⁹ Write therefore the things which you have seen, and the things which are, and the things which will happen hereafter; ²⁰ the mystery of the seven stars which you saw in my right hand, and the seven golden lamp stands. The seven stars are the angels of the seven assemblies. The seven lamp stands are seven assemblies."'

When John had his vision of Jesus, he was on the island of Patmos, which is a small island off the western coast of Turkey. Patmos was a prison quarry where the Roman empire sent its political prisoners to work in the mines. Tradition tells us that John was sent there in 94 or 95 AD while Domitian was the Roman emperor, and released in 96 or 97 AD after Domitian had died and Nerva had replaced him. Tradition also tells us that John then ministered in the area of Ephesus until he died a few years later, and was buried in Ephesus; the only apostle to die of old age. He would have been close to 90 years old then, if he'd been a young man following Jesus. John tells us what his crime was in verse 9. He says he was there, "because of the word of God and the testimony about Jesus." He had been arrested for his preaching about God because it was seen as a threat to the stability of Rome.

After all, if you have a religion that says your ultimate allegiance is to a God who you can't see, to whom no statues or temples are built, and this God is so jealous that He won't allow you to worship any other God; and whose followers would rather go to their death than do what they're told if it conflicts with what they feel that God is telling them to do: you have no power over such kinds of people. This is anarchy! What if it spread like a disease, and everyone becomes Christian? If you were a Roman official, you'd have no control over the populace. No army is big enough to defeat an overwhelming crowd of determined people. Such a disease could even infect the army itself, and then the power of the emperor would crumble. When the preaching of Christianity is seen from that perspective, it's a wonder John was merely in exile, rather than being executed on the spot. We do know from reading in the book of Acts about the Apostle Paul's two-year stay in Ephesus, that many people in Ephesus had been converted to Christianity, and that the officials there treated the Christians fairly, so maybe that's why John was only sent to prison on Patmos and released after only a few years, rather than being executed as were the rest of the apostles.

John introduces this section by saying four things about himself: he is a brother to those he's writing to, but he also shares in their suffering. The Greek word here for partner or companion comes from the word *koinonia*, which means "fellowship." Prefixed to *koinonia* is the word *sun*, which means "together." So John is saying he's fellowshipping together with his brothers in Christ in their suffering. The Greek word for suffering, *thlipsis*, means tribulation. He's suffering together with them under the tribulation brought about by the Roman government. Christians are being sought out and brought to trial, punishment, and death; and so is he. He's been through the trial, been sent to this rocky prison island, an ancient Alcatraz, and he spends his days breaking rock in the mines with a pickaxe, and remember, he's close to 90 years old. He wants them to know that this is not a letter from somebody who's living the good life on some Mediterranean resort. When he talks about tribulation, he knows it first hand.

But he goes on to say he's also fellowshipping with them in the Kingdom. They're all members of God's Kingdom, called by Jesus Christ to share in the life eternal that begins right here on earth. And then he goes on to say that he's also fellowshipping with them in patience. Sometimes when the troubles of the world are piled high on your plate, and there doesn't seem to be any relief in sight, you've just got to be patient. There have been many times when I've said to God, "How long, O Lord," and it's just been a matter of waiting. For John's brothers and sisters in Christ who may have been longing for the day when the Lord would return in judgment, the word from John is "Join me in being patient. The Lord is coming. Maybe I don't know exactly when, but all the promises of scripture, all the promises of Jesus himself, tell me that he could come at any time. Hang in there."

Jesus' word to us is "Hang in there." Now sometimes, that doesn't seem like a lot of comfort, because the problems that face us can be pretty big: a marriage that's struggling, kids that are in trouble, a job that looks like it might disappear tomorrow, or health that's failing. Pretty big problems. But John gives us a vision of Jesus that's not only equal to all our problems, but a whole lot bigger.

In verse 11, John hears a voice telling him to write everything he sees in a book to send to the churches. Turning around he sees seven golden lamps and in the middle stands someone like a son of man; not just a <u>man</u>, but a figure very similar to a man. "Son of Man" in verse 13 is a title for the Messiah, who receives power from God to rule over kings and kingdoms. Before John lets us know who this man is, he describes him in terms that would call to mind all the prophecies of Daniel about the heavenly Messiah. Read Daniel 7:13-14 again to see the parallels.

> *13 "I saw in the night visions, and behold, there came with the clouds of the sky one like a son of man, and he came even to the ancient of days, and they brought him near before him. 14 Dominion was given him, and glory, and a kingdom, that all the peoples, nations, and languages should serve him. His dominion is an everlasting dominion, which will not pass away, and his kingdom that which will not be destroyed." (Daniel 7:13-14)*

Revelation 1:13 says this figure in John's vision is clothed in a robe that goes all the way to his feet, and around his chest is a golden girdle. This is just like the description of the High priests in the Old Testament, and it would have reminded his readers of Daniel's description of a heavenly visitor in Daniel 10:5-6, 9 and 19.

> *5 "I lifted up my eyes, and looked, and behold, there was a man clothed in linen, whose thighs were adorned with pure gold of Uphaz. 6 His body also was like the beryl, and his face as the appearance of lightning, and his eyes*

as flaming torches. His arms and his feet were like burnished bronze. The voice of his words was like the voice of a multitude....⁹ When I heard the voice of his words, then I fell into a deep sleep on my face, with my face toward the ground....¹⁹ He said, "Greatly beloved man, don't be afraid. Peace be to you. Be strong. Yes, be strong." (Daniel 10:5-6, 9, 19)

Notice the shining face and the eyes like flaming torches, just like in Revelation. Note also the legs of burnished bronze, just like in Revelation, and the voice with the sound of a multitude, which is parallel to the voice of rushing waters in Revelation. In Daniel 10:9, Daniel falls to the ground, but the figure touches him and lifts him up, and then in verse 19 tells him not to be afraid, just like happens to John on Patmos. Daniel's vision and John's are of the same powerful heavenly person. In Daniel, this heavenly man goes on to explain what will happen to the kings of the earth and the people of God, and we find him performing the same role here in Revelation although the prophecies are different, because the situations are different.

In Revelation 1:18, we find that this heavenly person calls himself the "first and the last," which is equivalent to the "Alpha and Omega" in verse 8. In other words, he's equating himself to God the Father, the Ancient of Days, the Lord Almighty. This man is also the one who lives, even though he died; now, he's alive for ever more, which reveals to us that this heavenly figure is the resurrected Jesus. He goes on to say that he holds the keys to death and Hades. He's been there and come out the other side. The power of life and death is not in the hands of any earthly judge, or any earthly king or emperor. Jesus is in charge of how long you live, and when you will die. John is telling his friends in the churches of Asia not to worry when soldiers come knocking at your door. If they haul you off to court on the charges of being Christian, and you're sentenced to die, they don't hold the power over you. Jesus holds those keys, and he's the power who says you live or die, and if you die, he's just calling you home to be with him. Your life doesn't end, it's eternal. It continues on, just as Jesus died and yet lives for ever more.

How big is your concept of Jesus? Oral Roberts once reported a vision of a 700-foot-tall Jesus, and he was moved to build a medical school for his university. In verse 16, John saw a bright shining Jesus with a sword coming out of his mouth. This is quite a picture, like the illustration at the beginning of this chapter. One of the challenges in interpreting the book of Revelation is deciding exactly which details in all the fantastic images we read should be taken literally and which should we take figuratively? Does this picture mean that the heavenly Jesus goes around with a two-edged sword coming out of his mouth, so that when we get to heaven, we can't even get near him to give him a big hug without getting hurt? Or does it mean that the heavenly Jesus has the power of the sword, whether it's the two-edged sword used to separate truth from falsehood, as we find in the book of Hebrews 4:12, or a sword that can be used to attack and destroy the enemies of God? I think it's both. John is telling us that Jesus has the power and might of heaven at his disposal, and we're going to see him battling against the power of sin and evil, against Satan and all who support him, and Jesus will win. This is not the Jesus, meek and mild, the gentle shepherd, that we may have sung about in children's Sunday School. This is the figure of a mighty warrior on a gigantic scale, the Son of Man come in judgment as promised in Daniel.

In verse 16, the Son of Man holds seven stars in his right hand corresponding to the seven lamp stands. The heavenly Jesus explains to John in verse 20 that the seven stars are the angels of the seven churches listed in verse 11, and the seven lamp stands are those seven churches. The Greek word translated angel is *angelos. Angelos* means "messenger" and was frequently used in the secular world as a title for someone sent by an important official with an announcement or message. Angels are important figures throughout the book of Revelation. Chapter 5 records millions of angels gathered around God's throne praising the Lamb that was slain. But in verse 20 and in the next two chapters, the angels may not be heavenly beings, but may instead refer to human messengers entrusted with carrying this letter to the churches of verse 11.

Consider the possibility that this letter might have been sent to a regional gathering of the early churches, where messengers from each of the seven churches had come together to discuss common concerns. A delegate arrives from Patmos carrying copies of John's letter to be given to each messenger to be taken back to their home church and read to the entire congregation. So the messenger carrying this message of hope would arrive in one of the seven cities to be named in chapters 2 and 3 and look for the meeting place where the Christians would assemble on the first day of the week to deliver or read John's words of encouragement that he heard from Jesus. In the next two chapters, we'll see that each messenger is given a slightly different message that applies to each church's unique situation as they struggle to live in a hostile culture.

STUDY QUESTIONS

Q: How comforting do you think it would be to know that God is in charge, if you were being persecuted for your faith?

Q: If you received a letter in the mail like the Revelation, what might be your reaction?

Q: If you knew that eternal life had already begun for you, would it make a difference in how you lived?

Q: If you had been a Christian in one of these churches, what difference would it have made if John had said he was an apostle writing to you, instead of saying he was a brother writing to you?

Q: If you could picture Jesus as the powerful image we see in Revelation, rather than the picture of him as a shepherd that we see in Sunday School material, how might that change the way you live at work or home?

JESUS' MESSAGES TO THE CHURCHES, PT. 1

Chapters 2 and 3 contain individual letters addressed to seven churches of western Turkey, which was called Asia in the first century. Some people see these short letters as snapshots of the spiritual condition of the church throughout history up to the present time, but I think it's a lot easier to assume that they are pictures of actual first century churches and the problems they faced. When we interpret Revelation, we shouldn't let ourselves be distracted by all the visions that follow, and treat the entire book as if it were the predictions of a Nostradamus or Jeanne Dixon. Revelation is a letter to churches whose message and mission were opposed by other religions and by the state. It is a message of hope, not a message to terrify the weak, nor a prophecy of the total annihilation of the world. It is a message about the defeat of evil, and God's re-creation of a perfect world where oppression, fear, and sin no longer hold sway. Let's look at Revelation 2:1-7 to see what the heavenly Jesus says, both good and bad, to the church in Ephesus.

REVELATION 2:1-7

1 "To the angel of the assembly in Ephesus write: "He who holds the seven stars in his right hand, he who walks among the seven golden lamp stands says these things: 2 "I know your works, and your toil and perseverance, and that you can't tolerate evil men, and have tested those who call themselves apostles, and they are not, and found them false. 3 You have perseverance and have endured for my name's sake, and have not grown weary. 4 But I have this against you, that you left your first love. 5 Remember therefore from where you have fallen, and repent and do the first works; or else I am coming to you swiftly, and will move your lamp stand out of its place, unless you repent. 6 But this you have, that you hate the works of the Nicolaitans, which I also hate. 7 He who has an ear, let him hear what the Spirit says to the assemblies. To him who overcomes I will give to eat from the tree of life, which is in the Paradise of my God."

Each of the seven letters begins with a different part of John's vision of Christ in Chapter 1. Each letter ends with the phrase, "He who has an ear, let him hear what the Spirit says to the churches (assemblies)." In other words, just like each letter begins with a part of the vision of Jesus, each church is part of the church universal; none of them stands complete alone. What Christ says to each church, He's saying to them all, and to us as well, since we are also part of the church universal.

EPHESUS

The letter to the Ephesian church in Revelation chapter 2 starts out by saying that these are the words of him "who holds the seven stars in his right hand (and) walks among the seven golden lamp stands" which refers back to the image of Jesus that John saw in chapter 1. In verse 2, Jesus through John tells the church at Ephesus that He knows their hard work and their perseverance. But then in verse 4, He says that they have forsaken their first love. It's like a report card. The Ephesians get an A for effort, and an F for forgetting what's really important. From Acts 18:18-21, we learn how the church at Ephesus was started.

¹⁸ "Paul, having stayed after this many more days, took his leave of the brothers, and sailed from there for Syria, together with Priscilla and Aquila. He shaved his head in Cenchreae, for he had a vow. ¹⁹ He came to Ephesus, and he left them there; but he himself entered into the synagogue, and reasoned with the Jews. ²⁰ When they asked him to stay with them a longer time, he declined; ²¹ but taking his leave of them, he said, "I must by all means keep this coming feast in Jerusalem, but I will return again to you if God wills." Then he set sail from Ephesus. (Acts 18:18-21)

Paul left Corinth on his second journey through the Mediterranean regions headed back to Antioch, and along the way he stopped off in Ephesus. Here, he preached in the synagogue before moving on to Antioch, leaving behind Priscilla and Aquila. Meanwhile, Luke tells us that Apollos came to Ephesus, and that Priscilla and Aquila took him aside and taught him more about the Christian faith. Down in verse Acts 18:28, we find that Apollos then preached Jesus Christ to the Jewish people in Ephesus. Later on, in Acts chapter 19, Paul returned to Ephesus by land, and came back to the same synagogue, where he preached for three months. Opposition arose, so Paul moved to the lecture hall of Tyrannus, where he continued to preach about Jesus to both Jews and Greeks for another two years. So the church in Ephesus had enjoyed Paul's teaching during its formative years.

In Revelation 2:2, Jesus goes on to say that He knows the deeds of the church at Ephesus. He knows their hard work, and their perseverance. These are hardworking Christians. They spend hours working for Christ, spreading the gospel and taking care of the poor and needy. These are good, solid, church members. He praises them that they have had absolutely no patience for wicked men, and thoroughly test everyone who claims to be sent from God as an apostle, and reject the fakes. If David Koresh of Waco or Jim Jones of Guyana had come to the church at Ephesus, and told them he had been sent by God, he'd have been thrown out. The Ephesian Christians knew their theology, backwards and forwards. It had been strengthened by the teachings of Priscilla and Aquila, who had gotten it straight from Paul, and the Ephesian church allowed no deviation. Even when their faithful adherence to the truth got them into trouble with the authorities in Ephesus, they had endured whatever hardship, as it says in verse 3, and had not grown weary.

In spite of all the good things Jesus says about the church at Ephesus, what He says next tells us that they had lost a most important characteristic, that critical and essential quality that makes a church Christian, rather than just any kind of church: It's LOVE. Most scholars translate verse 4 as "you have left the love you had at first." Apparently, the church at Ephesus had worked themselves into a rigid orthodoxy that could instantly point out right from wrong, but had left behind the love of God and each other that is the true mark of Christians. Paul in I Corinthians 13:2 says that "if I have a faith which will move mountains but have not love, I am nothing." The Ephesians had a mountain-moving kind of faith, but they had lost the love that allows one person to accept another person as a fellow sinner saved only by God's grace, rather than by hard work. Because of that, their good works and their rigid adherence to what was right amounted to nothing. Jesus says in verse 5, "Repent, and do the works you did before. If you don't, I will come to you and move your lamp stand out of its place."

Imagine yourself a member of the Ephesian church as this was read from the pulpit. "Remove our lamp stand? That means if we do not change, we will no longer be part of the church universal. God himself will kick us out, close our doors, remove His Spirit from us. It's not fair! We've worked so hard to be righteous and true." But what God wants is balance in our faith. If we put all our emphasis on following a rigid set of rules and forget love, we have missed the heart of the Gospel.

God wants us to be open to the leading of His Spirit, which means we can't be rigid, we have to have a balanced flexibility and be willing to adjust to change that He brings to our lives. But does that flexibility mean we can do whatever we like, that there aren't any rules for Christians? Absolutely not; there is a difference between balance and flexibility. The Nicolaitans that we read about in verse 6 preached flexibility. We don't know exactly what their practices were, but scholars conclude that they were members of the churches of Asia who apparently taught, among other things, "We need to merge our Christian faith with what people around us believe, so that we'll be more acceptable. We can go to the temple of Artemis as long as we worship God in church on Sunday. And, if that includes eating sacred meals in the temple, or having sex with the temple prostitutes, it really doesn't matter, because we don't see that as worship of Artemis, even if others do." But how we live does matter to God, who hates any form of idolatry. Jesus commends the Ephesian church for rejecting those who would like to call themselves Christians, but who are willing to compromise their faith in God with the idolatrous practices of the culture.

Jesus concludes this short letter to the Ephesians by saying in verse 7, "To the one who overcomes, I will give the right to eat of the tree of life, which is in the paradise of God." That takes us back to the Garden of Eden in Genesis 2:8 and Adam and Eve. There were two particular trees in the center of that garden: the tree of knowledge of good and evil, from which they were to never eat, and another one, the tree of life, from which they could eat. As soon as they had eaten from the first one, God drove them out of the garden lest they continue to eat of the tree of life and live sinfully forever. The Rabbis taught that when the Messiah came, he would bring back the tree of life for God's people to eat from for eternity. The promise to the Ephesians is that if they heed Christ's warning; if they remember the love they had lost, if they repent, and return to sharing the love they had known when they first became Christians, then they would be showered with all the abundant life that God has to give his people.

SMYRNA

Jesus' letter to the church in Smyrna contains both compliments and challenges. Let's look at what they are.

REVELATION 2:8-11

8 "To the angel of the assembly in Smyrna write: "The first and the last, who was dead, and has come to life says these things: 9 "I know your works, oppression, and your poverty (but you are rich), and the blasphemy of those who say they are Jews, and they are not, but are a synagogue of Satan. 10 Don't be afraid of the things

which you are about to suffer. Behold, the devil is about to throw some of you into prison, that you may be tested; and you will have oppression for ten days. Be faithful to death, and I will give you the crown of life.
[11] He who has an ear, let him hear what the Spirit says to the assemblies. He who overcomes won't be harmed by the second death."

Smyrna and the church at Philadelphia in chapter 3 are the only ones about which the heavenly Christ has only good things to say. There's nothing negative here. They were doing everything that He expected them to do. But note that they are not big and successful, like the church at Ephesus, about whom Jesus had both kind and harsh words. These two are small and struggling. Smyrna was poor, while Philadelphia had little power and influence.

In verse 8, Jesus says He is "the first and the last," which is again a reference back to the vision of Jesus that John had in chapter 1, verse 17. In other words, He's the beginning and the end, and encompasses everything in between. For those persecuted Christians in Smyrna who were wondering whether this oppression would ever cease, Jesus lets them know that He's in control of time itself. He was there at creation of the world, and He'll be there at the re-creation of the world. I want you to notice that there's a parallel in the way this letter to Smyrna opens and closes. Jesus says He's the one who died and came to life again. Death wasn't the final curtain in His life. And then in verse 11, He promises those who overcome the fears and temptations to deny Him, that they will never be hurt by the second death.

What is this second death? Well, it comes after the first death, which comes to all of us. After we die physically, there comes a time of judgment when we either continue to live in heavenly bliss, or spiritually die what must seem a thousand deaths. It used to be popular to think that St. Peter meets you at the pearly gates and looks up in his book if you've been good or bad and decides whether to let you into heaven or send you to hell. I've heard some people say that everyone gets into heaven, no matter what, although maybe Adolf Hitler doesn't make it. But neither of these are the Biblical understanding of the judgment after our first death. The second death is a reality, and it comes to those who, when given the opportunity to give their lives to Jesus Christ, chose not to. Those folk would rather seize life for themselves and control it without interference rather than yield it to God; and for them there is a second death. This life — these 70 or 80 short years — are all we get to make that decision for Christ. After the first death comes, there's no opportunity to wish we had accepted Jesus as our Savior and Lord.

But, what is said about the Jews in verse 9 seems incredibly harsh. Why were they called liars and belonging to a synagogue of Satan? From the beginning, Jesus was seen by his followers as the Messiah fulfilling all the prophecies of the Old Testament. It was inconceivable to his followers that other Jewish people wouldn't see it that way too. But for most Jews, the concept of a Messiah dying on a cross was inconceivable, let alone any notion that he was divine.

When early Christian evangelists traveled to new cities, since they were Jewish themselves, they started teaching about Christ in synagogues, as Paul did. While many Jews, and Gentiles who also attended, showed interest, eventually the Christians were asked to leave. Jews had been given special permission by the Roman emperors to worship God and not worship the emperor. No other religion except Judaism had that special privilege. When Christians were no longer considered part of Judaism, Christianity was no longer protected, and became an illegal religion because it taught that worshipping the emperor was wrong. To make matters worse, Jews often were responsible for letting the Roman authorities know where Christians could be found. In fact, on one Sabbath Day in 155 AD, the Jews of Smyrna helped build the fire to burn Polycarp, the Christian Bishop of Smyrna.

Apparently, Jews were worried that Christians threatened their own survival. Ever since their return from Babylonian captivity, the Jews had met in synagogues and referred to their worship meetings as synagogues of God. Because of their involvement in turning Christians over to the Romans and rejecting Jesus as the Messiah, the Christians saw Jews conversely as synagogues of Satan.

All through the Old Testament were promises of a coming Messiah, however, who would climax the witness of the Jewish people by setting up a worldwide kingdom of peace centered around the worship of God. It was an eager expectation on many peoples' minds and hearts. That's the witness of the songs given in the book of Luke that were sung by Zechariah, the father of John the Baptist (Luke 1:68-79), and the old man Simeon in the Temple, when he heard about the birth of Jesus (Luke 2:29-32). While some of the Jewish people became followers of Jesus before and after his death and resurrection, many didn't, as we see here in the letter to Smyrna. Rejecting Jesus the Messiah was and is the ultimate rejection of God's purpose in choosing the Jews to be His chosen people. In other words, a Jewish person who rejects Jesus the Messiah, is no different than any other person who rejects Jesus the

Messiah. He or she puts themselves outside of God's kingdom by that choice. True Jews, then, are those who have accepted Jesus as Messiah, as Paul explains in his letter to the Romans chapters 10 and 11.

We are given a lot of choices in life. Choosing to be a Christian in our modern world is not the easiest choice to make. In Revelation 2:10, John tells the church in Smyrna that they will be undergoing persecution. Some of them will be put in prison and tested. He says they will suffer persecution for ten days. Now "ten days" struck me as unusual, because frequently when you went to prison in those days, you didn't come out alive. How could John be so precise? Why not seven days, since the number seven seems to be so important to John? Why not 40 days, since that's also a Biblical number. Most scholars just say that "ten days" is a way of saying "a short time", but I think that John is referring back to the example of Daniel and his friends, and their experience in the court of Nebuchadnezzer. Look at Daniel 1:3-20 to read about Daniel's training program in Babylon.

> *3 "The king spoke to Ashpenaz the master of his eunuchs, that he should bring in some of the children of Israel, even of the royal offspring and of the nobles; 4 youths in whom was no defect, but well-favored, and skillful in all wisdom, and endowed with knowledge, and understanding science, and who had the ability to stand in the king's palace; and that he should teach them the learning and the language of the Chaldeans. 5 The king appointed for them a daily portion of the king's dainties, and of the wine which he drank, and that they should be nourished three years; that at its end they should stand before the king. 6 Now among these were of the children of Judah: Daniel, Hananiah, Mishael, and Azariah. 7 The*

prince of the eunuchs gave names to them: to Daniel he gave the name Belteshazzar; to Hananiah, Shadrach; to Mishael, Meshach; and to Azariah, Abednego. ⁸ But Daniel purposed in his heart that he would not defile himself with the king's dainties, nor with the wine which he drank. Therefore he requested of the prince of the eunuchs that he might not defile himself. ⁹ Now God made Daniel find kindness and compassion in the sight of the prince of the eunuchs. ¹⁰ The prince of the eunuchs said to Daniel, "I fear my lord the king, who has appointed your food and your drink. For why should he see your faces worse looking than the youths who are of your own age? So would you endanger my head with the king."

¹¹ Then Daniel said to the steward whom the prince of the eunuchs had appointed over Daniel, Hananiah, Mishael, and Azariah: ¹² "Test your servants, I beg you, ten days; and let them give us vegetables to eat, and water to drink. ¹³ Then let our faces be examined before you, and the face of the youths who eat of the king's dainties; and as you see, deal with your servants." ¹⁴ So he listened to them in this matter, and tested them for ten days. ¹⁵ At the end of ten days, their faces appeared fairer, and they were fatter in flesh, than all the youths who ate of the king's dainties. ¹⁶ So the steward took away their dainties, and the wine that they would drink, and gave them vegetables. ¹⁷ Now as for these four youths, God gave them knowledge and skill in all learning and wisdom; and Daniel had understanding in all visions and dreams. ¹⁸ At the end of the days which the king had appointed for bringing them in, the prince of the eunuchs brought them in before Nebuchadnezzar. ¹⁹ The king talked with them; and among them all was found no one like Daniel, Hananiah, Mishael, and

Azariah. Therefore stood they before the king. [20] In every matter of wisdom and understanding, concerning which the king inquired of them, he found them ten times better than all the magicians and enchanters who were in all his realm." (Daniel 1:3-20)

Daniel, known as Belteshazar in Babylonian, Shadrach, Meshach, and Abednego, were selected for the management training program of the day. One of the perks of their three year course of study was the same food and wine that was served to the king. But this food was probably made from meat that had been offered to Marduk, the Babylonian god, and Daniel and his friends decided that eating such food would defile them, because they felt it would be an act of worship to Marduk to eat it. So they persuaded their overseer to feed them only vegetables and water. When the overseer protested he would lose his own head if his pupils lost weight and strength, Daniel told him to put it to a ten day test. Ten days to see if honoring God would be any more or less healthy than honoring Marduk. At the end of ten days, Daniel and his friends were healthier than the others, so they were allowed to continue in their menu, refrain from worshipping Marduk, and become advisors to the king.

The point of this ten day reference is that to survive in this world, you are commonly expected to live as everyone else does, to do what the king or government commands, even if it violates your religious principles. But, God says, if you do what you know is right and honoring to Me, you will enjoy eternal life in My kingdom, even if you don't survive in the world's kingdom. So, Jesus says in Revelation 2:10, "Be faithful unto death, and I will give you the crown of life." John is telling the church at Smyrna that they are going to be given the same choice as Daniel, worship God or worship Caesar. If they choose to worship God as Daniel did, and come through it, they will receive the crown of life, which is eternal life in the Kingdom of God.

PERGAMUM AND THYATIRA

The churches at Pergamum and Thyatira had a lot in common. Let's read their letters together to see the similarities.

REVELATION 2:12-29

¹² "To the angel of the assembly in Pergamum write: "He who has the sharp two-edged sword says these things: ¹³ "I know your works and where you dwell, where Satan's throne is. You hold firmly to my name, and didn't deny my faith in the days of Antipas my witness, my faithful one, who was killed among you, where Satan dwells. ¹⁴ But I have a few things against you, because you have there some who hold the teaching of Balaam, who taught Balak to throw a stumbling block before the children of Israel, to eat things sacrificed to idols, and to commit sexual immorality. ¹⁵ So you also have some who hold to the teaching of the Nicolaitans likewise. ¹⁶ Repent therefore, or else I am coming to you quickly, and I will make war against them with the sword of my mouth. ¹⁷ He who has an ear, let him hear what the Spirit says to the assemblies. To him who overcomes, to him I will give of the hidden manna, and I will give him a white stone, and on the stone a new name written, which no one knows but he who receives it.

¹⁸ "To the angel of the assembly in Thyatira write: "The Son of God, who has his eyes like a flame of fire, and his feet are like burnished brass, says these things:

[19] *"I know your works, your love, faith, service, patient endurance, and that your last works are more than the first.* [20] *But I have this against you, that you tolerate your woman, Jezebel, who calls herself a prophetess. She teaches and seduces my servants to commit sexual immorality, and to eat things sacrificed to idols.* [21] *I gave her time to repent, but she refuses to repent of her sexual immorality.* [22] *Behold, I will throw her into a bed, and those who commit adultery with her into great oppression, unless they repent of her works.* [23] *I will kill her children with Death, and all the assemblies will know that I am he who searches the minds and hearts. I will give to each one of you according to your deeds.* [24] *But to you I say, to the rest who are in Thyatira, as many as don't have this teaching, who don't know what some call 'the deep things of Satan,' to you I say, I am not putting any other burden on you.* [25] *Nevertheless, hold that which you have firmly until I come.* [26] *He who overcomes, and he who keeps my works to the end, to him I will give authority over the nations.* [27] *He will rule them with a rod of iron, shattering them like clay pots; as I also have received of my Father:* [28] *and I will give him the morning star.* [29] *He who has an ear, let him hear what the Spirit says to the assemblies."*

While the churches of Pergamum and Thyatira had a lot in common, the cities themselves did not. Pergamum was the capital city of the province. It was big and wealthy, and was the center of the worship of Zeus, the head god of the Greek and Roman pantheon, and the center of emperor worship in the area. Thyatira was a small city 40 miles away, known for its craftsmen and trade guilds. Lydia, the dealer in purple cloth that the Apostle Paul met in Philippi was from Thyatira.

Again, the opening words of each of these short letters comes from the powerful image of the resurrected Christ that John told us about in Chapter 1. In verse 12, the church at Pergamum is reminded that Christ has a double-edged sword, that not only can separate truth from falsehood, but also be used to destroy God's enemies. In verse 18, the church at Thyatira is reminded that Christ is the Son of God, bright and shining with the power of God behind him. Back in verse 13, Jesus, through John, says that Pergamum is the place where Satan has his throne. He's telling the Christians there that he understands how hard it is to stay true to the faith in Pergamum, the center of the worship of both Zeus and the emperor Trajan, who ruled from 98-117 AD. But Jesus goes on to say that in spite of the persecution, even the martyrdom of Antipas, He knows they have not renounced their faith in him. In Thyatira, Jesus says in verse 19, He knows their deeds, and how they've loved, and served, and persevered, and even in the midst of persecution, have done even more than they used to. They haven't shrunk away and hid. They've kept at it, and worked even harder.

But in both churches, there are problems. In Pergamum, in verse 14, we read that there are some in the church who were following the teachings of Balaam, a prophet of Moab in the Old Testament who opposed the people of God. In verse 15, we find that some others in the church are following the teachings of the Nicolaitans. And in Thyatira, in verse 20, we read about a self-proclaimed prophetess in the church, who Jesus calls Jezebel after the evil wife of King Ahab in the Old Testament. All these splinter groups had two things in common: they were accused of eating food offered to idols, and participating in sexual immorality. And these weren't just rumors; these folk were proud of their behavior and taught it as something OK for Christians to do.

The apostle Paul had written about these issues 40 years earlier in his first letter to the Corinthian church. Look at I Corinthians 10:18-21 to see what Paul said about eating food sacrificed to idols.

18 "Consider Israel according to the flesh. Don't those who eat the sacrifices participate in the altar? 19 What am I saying then? That a thing sacrificed to idols is anything, or that an idol is anything? 20 But I say that the things which the Gentiles sacrifice, they sacrifice to demons, and not to God, and I don't desire that you would have fellowship with demons. 21 You can't both drink the cup of the Lord and the cup of demons. You can't both partake of the table of the Lord, and of the table of demons." (I Corinthians 10:18-21)

The question had come up in the Corinthian church, which was in Greece, about eating the meat offered to idols, and Paul said that although we Christians know that it doesn't really mean anything, if you know that it was involved in idol worship, don't eat it. Look at I Corinthians 10:28 to see another reason not to eat food offered to idols.

28 "But if anyone says to you, "This was offered to idols," don't eat it for the sake of the one who told you, and for the sake of conscience. For "the earth is the Lord's, and all its fullness." (I Corinthians 10:28)

The reason is not to confuse anyone about who you really worship. Don't let them think you still worship Artemis or Zeus after you've become a Christian and are telling people there is only one God. It's confusing. And it weakens your message.

Paul also addressed the issue of sexual immorality in I Corinthians 6:15-16, and this is specifically focused at the issue of temple prostitutes.

15 "Don't you know that your bodies are members of Christ? Shall I then take the members of Christ, and make them members of a prostitute? May it never be! 16 Or don't you know that he who is joined to a prostitute is one body? For, "The two", he says, "will become one flesh." (I Corinthians 6:15-16)

Paul refers to Genesis 2:24, "The two will become one flesh," to say that sex is not just a casual affair or a recreational activity. When you become a Christian, you are one with God, and you can't extend that oneness to include the worship of another god through the use of a temple prostitute. Christianity was diametrically opposed to the Greek and Roman culture when Christianity said you could only worship one God.

So that's why those in the church who were saying it doesn't matter if Christians participated in worship of other gods were wrong. It does matter. Christianity transcends culture, it should not be bound by it. What Paul said in Galatians 3:28 radically universalized culture: "There is neither Jew nor Greek, there is neither slave nor free man, there is neither male nor female; for you are all one in Christ Jesus." Paul's teaching was also revolutionary, because it attacked the economic system that was based on slavery. It undermined empires because it broke down the nationalistic animosities that the Roman armies played upon to keep the peace. Christianity opposed first century households by setting men and women on an equal plane.

In the end of these short letters to the Christians in Pergamum and Thyatira, Jesus promises several things to those who overcome their cultural temptations and stay true to Him, and that includes us as well. In verse 17, he promises some of the hidden manna, which is spiritual food provided by God himself, just like he provided it to the Hebrew slaves on their exodus to freedom. And he also promises a "white stone with a new name written on it that only the receiver knows." I believe this inscribed stone is like an invitation we'd receive to a wedding, and is addressed to us with a special name that we'll recognize when we see it. We are invited to join Jesus with all the other Christians in heaven at the grand celebration for those who've overcome. In verse 26, Jesus promises power and authority to those who are weak and powerless in this life, whether Christians in Thyatira, or those who are murdered today in Africa or China or the inner cities of America. But he also promises them the morning star, which we will discover in Revelation 22:16 is Jesus Christ himself. The morning star is that bright star you see in the morning, which brings hope to the world, because it means there's a new day dawning, a new day where the old ways can be reformed and forgotten and replaced by a new day filled with endless possibilities and opportunities. These are promises of hope to faithful Christians in every age: abundance and fellowship without pain, freedom from oppressive control, and the opportunity to make each day a new day.

JESUS' MESSAGES TO THE CHURCHES, PT. 2

Chapter 3 of the book of Revelation continues the short letters to seven of the churches in Asia (Western Turkey), in which the heavenly Jesus gives specific instructions to John for the churches of Sardis, Philadelphia and Laodicea. Sardis and Laodicea receive words of warning to repent and return to following Jesus, while Philadelphia receives words of encouragement to hang in there during the tough times. Each letter contains the familiar themes of promises of reward to those who overcome during persecution accompanied by assurances of an imminent return of the Lord in judgment on the wicked and support to the faithful.

Sardis at the beginning of chapter 3 and Laodicea at the end of chapter 3 are two similar churches in that they are great churches, big and rich, but it's all a big facade. Jesus calls Sardis "dead" and Laodicea "lukewarm." Not the words you'd like to have anybody use to describe your church. In the middle of chapter 3 lies little Philadelphia, the weakest, and yet more faithful than its larger and more successful neighbors.

SARDIS

Sardis was an interesting city. Remember Midas, the mythical king who had a magic touch so that everything he touched turned to gold? Well, Croesus, the king of Lydia in the sixth century BC, of which Sardis was the capital, was a real-life Midas because he had lots of gold and was very wealthy. Sardis was on a river from which gold was mined, and built on top of a sheer 1500 foot cliff next to the river that Croesus thought was the ultimate defense. No one could touch him and his gold. But Cyrus, the king of Persia, came and laid siege to Sardis in 549 BC. One of his soldiers climbed that sheer cliff, found no guards to stop him, and opened the gates of the city to Cyrus. Apparently, the same approach was used in 216 BC when Antiochus the Great also captured the city.

Read Revelation 3:1-6 to see what the heavenly Jesus says to the church at Sardis whose members need to repent and return to following their Lord.

REVELATION 3:1-6

¹ "And to the angel of the assembly in Sardis write: "He who has the seven Spirits of God, and the seven stars says these things: "I know your works, that you have a reputation of being alive, but you are dead. ² Wake up, and keep the things that remain, which you were about to throw away, for I have found no works of yours perfected before my God. ³ Remember therefore how you have received and heard. Keep it, and repent. If therefore you won't watch, I will come as a thief, and you won't know what hour I will come upon you. ⁴ Nevertheless you have a few names in Sardis that didn't defile their garments. They will walk with me in white, for they are worthy. ⁵ He who overcomes will be arrayed in white garments, and I will in no way blot his name out of the book of life, and I will confess his name before my Father, and before his angels. ⁶ He who has an ear, let him hear what the Spirit says to the assemblies."

So, when the heavenly Jesus says to the church at Sardis in verse 3 that they'd better repent, or he'd come as a thief in the night, they'd understand that no one is impregnable. Don't be sleeping like Sardis was when Cyrus and Antiochus came. "Wake up! Come to your senses," Jesus says. In verse 1, we find that the church had a reputation of being alive, but was really dead. The church was putting on a good impression for everybody to see. "Look, we're being good Christians, we're going to church, we're listening to the sermon, we're giving to the poor; so what's wrong?" In verse 2, Jesus says that he has not found their deeds complete in the sight of God. In other words, everything they do, they do half-heartedly. True faith had been replaced by appearances. A church like Sardis today might have a few projects in the community, but they're just for show, and don't have the support of most of the congregation. They might belong to the food shelf, but they don't contribute food or volunteers. They might contribute to missions, but no one's interested in what's happening in those missions because they are really more focused on themselves. These folk are going through the motions, as if it's a habit or a social nicety, not a way of life.

Verse 4 tells us that not everybody in the church at Sardis was there for the show. There were a few people there to whom faith and trust in the Lord was real and prayer was valued, and serving others in compassion meant giving of one's time and energy. And for them the risen Lord promises life eternal with Him in glory. In verse 4, He says they will walk with Him in white garments, to indicate the purity of their heavenly existence, as opposed to the soiled garments of earthly life. Some scholars think

Jesus is referring to resurrection bodies rather than earthly bodies when he talks about their white garments. In verse 5, that promise is extended to everyone who overcomes the temptation to make Christianity merely a put-on, but instead makes the Lordship of Christ real in their lives. Their names will be written in the book of life, and they will be acknowledged by Christ himself before the throne of God.

PHILADELPHIA

The church at Philadelphia has kept the faith even while undergoing persecution. Let's read what Jesus says to them.

REVELATION 3:7-13

7 "To the angel of the assembly in Philadelphia write: "He who is holy, he who is true, he who has the key of David, he who opens and no one can shut, and who shuts and no one opens, says these things: 8 "I know your works (behold, I have set before you an open door, which no one can shut), that you have a little power, and kept my word, and didn't deny my name. 9 Behold, I give some of the synagogue of Satan, of those who say they are Jews, and they are not, but lie. Behold, I will make them to come and worship before your feet, and to know that I have loved you. 10 Because you kept my command to endure, I also will keep you from the hour of testing, which is to come on the whole world, to test those who dwell on the earth. 11 I am coming quickly! Hold firmly that which you have, so that no one takes your crown. 12 He who overcomes, I will make him a pillar in the temple of my God, and he will go out from there no more. I will write on him the name of my God, and the name of the city of my God, the new Jerusalem, which comes down out of heaven from my God, and my own new name. ¹³ *He who has an ear, let him hear what the Spirit says to the assemblies."*

The message to the church at Philadelphia is similar to that of Smyrna in that Jesus has nothing but good things to say about it, but it's different in His promises to them. This letter starts out by saying that Jesus holds the Key of David, which opens the door which no one can shut, and shuts the door no one can open. This is a reference to Isaiah 22:20-22, where Eliakim is given the key to the house of David.

²⁰ *"It will happen in that day that I will call my servant Eliakim the son of Hilkiah,* ²¹ *and I will clothe him with your robe, and strengthen him with your belt. I will commit your government into his hand; and he will be a father to the inhabitants of Jerusalem, and to the house of Judah.* ²² *I will lay the key of David's house on his shoulder. He will open, and no one will shut. He will shut, and no one will open." (Isaiah 22:20-22)*

I believe this means Eliakim would have the power to decide who gets in to see the King, and who does not. Jesus tells the Christians in Philadelphia that the door to the Kingdom of God is open wide to them, and no earthly power can keep them out. The Jews that oppose them can't keep them out, and in fact will eventually acknowledge them as loved by God. Because they have not denied His name, as it says in verse 8, but have been enduring patiently, as it says in verse 10, they will be spared the persecution coming on the church. He tells them to hold on to what they have. Verse 12 concludes by saying that those who stay with Him and overcome the temptation to deny

Him and save their skins will become pillars in the temple of God. They will have written on them the name of God, the name of the new city of God, and His own new name. Having a name written on you is a way of indicating to whom you belong.

To the people in Ephesus, Jesus promised that if they overcame the temptation to join the rest of the world in paganism and immorality they will be given the right to eat forever from the tree of life in the middle of Paradise. To the people in Smyrna, Jesus promised to those who remain faithful and don't deny Him when life gets hard, that they will never see the second death reserved for those who do deny Him. To the people in Philadelphia, Jesus promised to those who patiently endure being rejected by the world because of their faith, that they will be marked as those who belong to Him. But these letters were written for all churches to read. So, these promises are for us, too, as we try to live our Christian faith in an increasingly non-Christian world.

LAODICEA

The heavenly Jesus says the Laodiceans are lukewarm and self-deceived in his letter to them. Let's look at it.

REVELATION 3:14-22

14 "To the angel of the assembly in Laodicea write: "The Amen, the Faithful and True Witness, the Beginning* of God's creation, says these things:

15 "I know your works, that you are neither cold nor hot. I wish you were cold or hot. 16 So, because you are lukewarm, and neither hot nor cold, I will vomit you out of my mouth. 17 Because you say, 'I am rich, and have gotten riches, and have need of nothing;' and don't know that you are the wretched one, miserable, poor, blind, and naked; ¹⁸ I counsel you to buy from me gold refined by fire, that you may become rich; and white garments, that you may clothe yourself, and that the shame of your nakedness may not be revealed; and eye salve to anoint your eyes, that you may see. ¹⁹ As many as I love, I reprove and chasten. Be zealous therefore, and repent. ²⁰ Behold, I stand at the door and knock. If anyone hears my voice and opens the door, then I will come in to him, and will dine with him, and he with me. ²¹ He who overcomes, I will give to him to sit down with me on my throne, as I also overcame, and sat down with my Father on his throne. ²² He who has an ear, let him hear what the Spirit says to the assemblies."

Laodicea was similar to Sardis, because it also had a church where faith had been replaced by something else, but rather than appearances and show, in this church their wealth was what they really trusted in. Both Sardis and Laodicea were destroyed by earthquakes in the first century. Sardis was rebuilt with money donated by the emperor Tiberias. The Laodiceans did it themselves. They were the wealthiest city in Phrygia. In verse 17, you can read them saying how rich they are. They got their wealth from three industries: wool, banking, and medicine. What Jesus says to the Laodiceans is full of irony. In verse 17, he counters their claim to be rich and in need of nothing, by saying that they are wretched, pitiful, poor, blind and naked. Instead of being wealthy, they are poor and to be pitied. Instead of being clothed with the premium wool garments Laodicea was famous for, they are naked. The famous eye-salve produced by their doctors was for nothing, because they are blind. Jesus tells them in verse 18 to come to Him for real wealth, the true riches of faith;

for white clothes of heaven instead of the black wool of their sheep; and find spiritual eye-salve that will allow them to see the truth of their neediness.

Because they trust their riches instead of Him, Jesus says in verse 15 that they are neither cold nor hot, but only lukewarm, and He will spit them out. They knew what He meant, because right opposite the city of Laodicea was the city of Hierapolis, known for its mineral hot springs. And only a few miles the other way was the city of Colossae situated on the bank of the river Lycus with its cold waters. Laodicea was neither hot like Hierapolis, nor cold like Colossae. It was literally in the middle. If you mix the mineral water from Hierapolis with the river water from Colossae, you have lukewarm water that tastes strongly of salt and alum. You'd spit it out, too, if you took a drink of it. It isn't any good to drink; you can't grow crops with it; it's not good for anything, just like the church at Laodicea.

In verse 19, Jesus tells them He still loves them and encourages them to repent. He hasn't left them, even though they may have stopped trusting Him and started trusting their riches. He holds out the promise of verse 20, "Behold, I stand at the door and knock. If anyone hears my voice and opens the door, I will come in to him and will dine with him, and he with me." Jesus is reaching out to people in Laodicea and anyone else who's tied up in their own busyness at making a buck, or wheeling a deal, or building a fortune, and offers Himself in fellowship. He's got time for you, even if you don't have time for Him.

These letters are addressed to the Christians in seven of the churches of Asia, but they're also pointed directly at us. The problems they faced are very similar to the problems we face today. The temptations they faced are

very similar to the temptations we face today. To those
Christians facing persecution like those in Ephesus,
Smyrna and Philadelphia, these letters offer the comfort of
a powerful Christ who will win over evil, and bring
Christians home to be with Him. To those Christians who
have compromised their faith with the popular religions of
the world like those at Pergamum and Thyatira, these
letters call for repentance and offer the comfort of
forgiveness with the strength to stand true. To those who
trust in their own strength and abilities like those at Sardis
and Laodicea, the patient Christ waits for their humble
return. To all who overcome, He holds out the promise of
an eternal life of fellowship with Him and the Father and
all the saints and angels in heaven.

In the next chapters of Revelation, John shares his
vision of God, and after that the tone of the book of
Revelation changes quite a bit. From now to the end of the
book, we'll find a series of visions of the world being
punished for its unbelief; of the defeat of Satan and his
accomplices; and the recreation of a new world where God
truly reigns.

STUDY QUESTIONS

Q: Given the background we read in Acts, what might we conclude about the church in Ephesus?

Q: What would you say is the most important characteristic of a great church, something you'd like people to say about your church?

Q: The letter to the church in Ephesus shows they didn't tolerate splinter groups as did Pergamum and Thyatira, but that they had lost the characteristic of love in the process. In which church would you feel most comfortable?

Q: What message should Christianity be bringing to our modern culture?

Q: Can you picture standing before God's throne, and having Christ stand by your side, and introduce you, "God, here's Joe. He's an overcomer." What would that feel like to you?

4

John's Vision of God on His Throne

John now experiences an awesome vision of God in heaven surrounded by the host of heaven and praised by representatives of believers throughout the ages.

Revelation 4:1-11

¹ "After these things I looked and saw a door opened in heaven, and the first voice that I heard, like a trumpet speaking with me, was one saying, "Come up here, and I will show you the things which must happen after this."

² Immediately I was in the Spirit. Behold, there was a throne set in heaven, and one sitting on the throne ³ that looked like a jasper stone and a sardius. There was a rainbow around the throne, like an emerald to look at. ⁴ Around the throne were twenty-four thrones. On the thrones were twenty-four elders sitting, dressed in white garments, with crowns of gold on their heads. ⁵ Out of the throne proceed lightnings, sounds, and thunders. There were seven lamps of fire burning before his throne, which are the seven Spirits of God. ⁶ Before the throne was something like a sea of glass, similar to crystal. In the middle of the throne, and around the throne were four living creatures full of eyes before and behind. ⁷ The first creature was like a lion, and the second creature like a calf, and the third creature had a

face like a man, and the fourth was like a flying eagle.
⁸ The four living creatures, each one of them having six
wings, are full of eyes around and within. They have no
rest day and night, saying, "Holy, holy, holy is the Lord
God, the Almighty, who was and who is and who is to
come!" ⁹ When the living creatures give glory, honor,
and thanks to him who sits on the throne, to him who
lives forever and ever, ¹⁰ the twenty-four elders fall
down before him who sits on the throne, and worship
him who lives forever and ever, and throw their crowns
before the throne, saying, ¹¹ "Worthy are you, our Lord
and God, the Holy One, to receive the glory, the honor,
and the power, for you created all things, and because of
your desire they existed, and were created!"

John, the writer of Revelation, was given the
opportunity to see God, and he tries to tell us in Chapter 4
what God is like. One of the reasons the images we see in
Revelation seem so hard to understand may be that John is
at a loss for words. How do you describe God, after all?
What does He look like? When God is talked about in the
Old Testament, the biblical writers do the best they can to
describe how God acts. They talk about His mighty arm
giving them protection. They talk about the light of His
face shining on them. They talk about the works of His
fingers. They talk about the breath of His nostrils. Now,
does God really have arms and hands and fingers, and a
face with ears and eyes and a nose, just like the artist
Michelangelo might have drawn? All through the Bible, we
are told that God is a spirit; God doesn't look like the
picture Michelangelo painted on the ceiling of the Sistine
chapel with a long white beard; He's not a human being
like we are.

But the Biblical writers had no other way to talk about God except in common ordinary words that we humans could relate to and understand. This is important to realize when we look at the image of God that John gives us, because he's trying his hardest to tell us what he saw, even though he has no human words that can describe the majesty of God. And so, he tries to paint a picture for us. You might say his painting in words looks more like a Picasso than a Michelangelo, because it's filled with vague images, using phrases like "had the appearance of" in verse 3, "looked like" in verse 6, "was like" in verse 7, "resembling" in verse 4. In other words, he's telling us this is not an exact picture of God, because he can only say it is similar to other things that his readers would understand. But he does know images from the Old Testament that meant a lot to God's people throughout the centuries, and his description of God on his throne has a lot of commonalities with the description of God on his throne that we find in the Old Testament, such as Ezekiel's vision of God.

28 *"As the appearance of the rainbow that is in the cloud in the day of rain, so was the appearance of the brightness all around. This was the appearance of the likeness of Yahweh's glory. When I saw it, I fell on my face, and I heard a voice of one that spoke." (Ezekiel 1:28)*

This last sentence of Ezekiel chapter 1 tells us that what comes before is the appearance of the likeness of the glory of the Lord. Again, the words "appearance" and "likeness" tell us that Ezekiel didn't have the words to describe exactly what he saw either, but could only paint a picture for us of his vision. Look at Ezekiel 1:4-12,22-28 to see Ezekiel's full description of his vision of God.

4 "I looked, and behold, a stormy wind came out of the
north: a great cloud, with flashing lightning, and a
brightness around it, and out of the middle of it as it
were glowing metal, out of the middle of the fire. 5 Out of
its center came the likeness of four living creatures. This
was their appearance: They had the likeness of a man.
6 Everyone had four faces, and each one of them had
four wings. 7 Their feet were straight feet. The sole of
their feet was like the sole of a calf's foot; and they
sparkled like burnished bronze. 8 They had the hands of
a man under their wings on their four sides. The four of
them had their faces and their wings like this: 9 Their
wings were joined to one another. They didn't turn when
they went. Each one went straight forward. 10 As for the
likeness of their faces, they had the face of a man. The
four of them had the face of a lion on the right side. The
four of them had the face of an ox on the left side. The
four of them also had the face of an eagle. 11 Such were
their faces. Their wings were spread out above. Two
wings of each one touched another, and two covered
their bodies. 12 Each one went straight forward: where
the spirit was to go, they went. They didn't turn when
they went. (Ezekiel 1:4-12)

22 "Over the head of the living creature there was the
likeness of an expanse, like an awesome crystal to look
at, stretched out over their heads above. 23 Under the
expanse, their wings were straight, one toward the
other. Each one had two which covered on this side, and
each one had two which covered their bodies on that
side. 24 When they went, I heard the noise of their wings
like the noise of great waters, like the voice of the
Almighty, a noise of tumult like the noise of an army.
When they stood, they let down their wings.

25 There was a voice above the expanse that was over their heads. When they stood, they let down their wings. 26 Above the expanse that was over their heads was the likeness of a throne, as the appearance of a sapphire§ stone. On the likeness of the throne was a likeness as the appearance of a man on it above. 27 I saw as it were glowing metal, as the appearance of fire within it all around, from the appearance of his waist and upward; and from the appearance of his waist and downward I saw as it were the appearance of fire, and there was brightness around him. 28 As the appearance of the rainbow that is in the cloud in the day of rain, so was the appearance of the brightness all around.

This was the appearance of the likeness of Yahweh's glory. When I saw it, I fell on my face, and I heard a voice of one that spoke." (Ezekiel 1:22-28)

Starting in verse 26, Ezekiel reports he saw a throne of sapphire, with a figure of a man, that glowed like metal, with fire and brilliant light around him. In verse 28, Ezekiel says the radiance around this figure was like a rainbow in the clouds on a rainy day. Look again at Revelation 4:2-3.

2 "Immediately I was in the Spirit. Behold, there was a throne set in heaven, and one sitting on the throne 3 that looked like a jasper stone and a sardius. There was a rainbow around the throne, like an emerald to look at." (Revelation 4:2-3)

We see a throne with someone sitting on it, with the appearance of semi-precious stones, and a rainbow circling around it. The sardius stone is better known today as carnelian, and is blood-red in color. John doesn't tell us anything at all about the shape of God, but only that He looks like the jewels you might associate with royalty. Also in verse 5 we find lighting and thunder coming from the area of the throne, which is similar to the fire and brilliant light in Ezekiel's vision. In other words, both John and Ezekiel are telling us that God is a source of tremendous energy, like looking into a blast furnace today, or a nuclear reactor.

The similarities between Ezekiel's and John's description of God on His throne go on. In Revelation 4:6, around the throne are four living creatures, covered with eyes. These creatures are described in verse 7 as like a lion, like an ox, one having a face like a man, and like a flying eagle. In Ezekiel 1:5, we see four living creatures, and in verse 10, we find that each of them had four faces: the face of a man, the face of a lion, the face of an ox, and the face of an eagle. The Rabbis said that these represented the best qualities in nature: man for intelligence, the lion for bravery, the ox for strength, and the eagle for swiftness. In

Revelation, each creature was different, having only one face, but in Ezekiel, each creature was the same, having four faces. In Ezekiel, these creatures have four wings, but in Revelation they have six wings. Later on in Ezekiel 10:1, these creatures are called the cherubim, which is the Hebrew plural for "cherub." I have to tell you, this is not what I thought cherubs looked like. They're not fat little angels with bows and arrows that help people fall in love. As described in both Revelation and Ezekiel, these are pretty awesome creatures, and they certainly wouldn't make it onto a valentine card.

There are more similarities between Revelation 4 and Ezekiel chapter 1. In Revelation 4:6, we find the throne is surrounded by something that looked like a sea of glass, clear as crystal, and in Ezekiel 1:22, we find an expanse that sparkles like ice. In Greek, the word crystal is *krustallo* which is the same word used for ice in the Greek version of Ezekiel. It's the same thing. I think this crystal sea or expanse may be a way of describing the infinity of heaven. But there are also some differences. In Ezekiel 1:15, Ezekiel says the living creatures were accompanied by wheels full of eyes, which were interlocked in some way, so that they didn't turn, but they moved. The eyes, which also appear in John's vision in Revelation 4:6, indicate God's ability to see and know all that's going on. God's not blind to the troubles of His people. The purpose of both visions is the same. God appeared to both these men during hard times for the people of God. In Ezekiel's day, they were in captivity in Babylon. In John's day, they were being persecuted by the Romans. In both situations, people needed to be encouraged to keep the faith, and those who had corrupted or given up their faith needed to repent and return to God. Both Ezekiel and John were given that task by the same God who appeared to both of them in very similar visions.

John's vision of God and Ezekiel's vision of God are essentially the same. I say that because of the similarities of their visions, the circumstances surrounding their visions, and the message that they were given in their visions to pass on. I think the differences we see are what you might expect from two people who experienced the same vision but found they had no words to describe exactly what they saw. So they tried to communicate as best they could in two different languages, Hebrew and Greek, by painting in words pictures of their encounter with God.

Returning to Revelation chapter 4, we can identify three major characteristics of God in John's vision. First is the <u>awesome majesty and power</u> of God seated on His throne of glory. God is the source of tremendous energy, and served by fantastic, awe-inspiring creatures representing God's creation, and also by representatives of God's people who have passed from death to life in the Heavenly realm. When you are up against the invincible power of Rome, you need to hear that God is even more powerful. The Roman armies seemed to be unbeatable. They were well organized, well disciplined, and expertly commanded. They had conquered the known world. The Roman emperors became satiated with power. The emperor Domitian, whose decree put John in prison, demanded that he be worshipped as "Our Lord and God." The local procurators and governors that he appointed throughout the empire were responsible for enforcing that worship. With the Roman army at their disposal to back them up, they possessed the ultimate power of life and death over their subjects. And yet, God's power is even greater. Rome's power crumbled because of its success. It became fat and happy, and the leadership declined into self-serving opulence and gratification. But it was also true that Christianity had a large part to play in Rome's decline, because Christianity broke down the barriers that separated people from each other. It was their love toward one another and love toward their enemies that broke the power of Rome. Earthly might has no power over love enabled by God's power.

The second characteristic that John focuses on is the holiness of God. In verse 8, the living creatures sing day and night "Holy, holy, holy is the Lord God Almighty, who was and is and is to come." Among other things, holiness means purity. God is truly righteous and pure. Everything He does is for our good. In contrast, the Roman emperor Domitian was not righteous and pure; nor was he interested in anyone's good but his own. God is eternal. He was and is and is to come—without limit, without end. Domitian, on the other hand, is only a man. He will die. In fact, within a year or two of the time of John's writing, Domitian was murdered by his wife and servants because of his evil. The lesson for John's readers is not to put your faith and trust in an earthly power that is here today and gone tomorrow, but to trust in God who reigns forever.

The third characteristic of God that John mentions is God's unique creative power. John tells us that twenty four elders surrounded God's throne, and took off their crowns and laid them at his feet. Who are these twenty four elders? Opinions vary, but many scholars say they are the combination of the leaders of the twelve tribes of Israel and the twelve apostles. Others say they are the New Testament equivalent to the heads of the 24 orders of priests in the Old Testament. In any case, these twenty four elders proclaim in verse 11 that God alone is worthy to receive glory and honor and power. Note that they say "Our Lord and God." Domitian who demanded to be called "Our Lord and God" and who demanded glory and honor and power, is <u>not</u> the object of their worship. Only the Almighty God is, because He alone created all things. Domitian didn't. And not only did God create all things, He sustains them—they continue to exist because of Him. God did not just put the universe in motion, like one might wind up an old clock, and let it go. He is alive and active in this world, and keeps it running. In this chapter of Revelation, John shares with us his vision of an all-powerful God, holy and merciful, loved and adored by His creation. This vision is a convincing message to those who believe: have patience and trust in the Almighty God who is coming to defeat evil and save His people. It's also a message to those who don't believe: don't trust in your earthly kingdoms and comfort, because God is coming in judgment. It's high time to repent and change where you've put your trust.

Now let's turn in the next chapter to another vision John has of Jesus receiving authority from God to carry out His plan.

JESUS: BOTH LION AND LAMB

To interpret the images of Revelation, we have to constantly turn back to the prophets of the Old Testament, particularly Ezekiel, Daniel, Isaiah, and Zechariah. Many of the prophets spoke in poetry rather than prose, which you can see in modern versions of the Old Testament by the way their sayings are formatted. Hebrew poetry is not like our poetry because it doesn't rhyme or worry about meter. Instead, Hebrew poets, including the prophets, used parallelism of thought, or contrasting thoughts, to make their points. Here are two examples of Hebrew poetry quoted in Revelation, the first example showing two lines with similar or parallel ideas expressed, and the second example showing two lines that have opposing or anti-parallel ideas expressed:

Parallelism of thought:
  "He will rule them with a rod of iron,
      shattering them like clay pots;"
          (Revelation 2:27, quoting Psalm 2:9)

Anti-parallel:
  "Therefore rejoice, heavens, and you who dwell in them.
      Woe to the earth and to the sea, because the devil has
          gone down to you,"
          (Revelation 12:12, quoting Psalm 96:11)

When you read poetry that was originally written in Hebrew, you don't dissect it into little bits in an attempt to figure out the thought or meaning behind each individual word or phrase. You take it as a whole, and try to picture what the poet is portraying in parallel or contrasting thought patterns. Chuck Swindoll uses the example of an artist and an engineer going to an art museum to explain the difference between Western and Hebrew poetry. An engineer might look at a modern painting and comment, "I don't get it; it doesn't make any sense; why did the artist do it that way?" His artist friend turns to the engineer and tells him to stop trying to analyze it; and let his senses and intuition discover what the artist was trying to communicate. Analysis can kill the meaning of art, just as it can poetry.

And that's the challenge for us as we study Revelation, not to lose the meaning by over-analyzing every image, but get the big picture. John is painting pictures for us in words. We have to stand back and grasp the whole, rather than dissect each individual detail. We can't allow ourselves to focus so tightly that we miss the bigger and more important meaning of the whole scene and what it means to our faith.

In Revelation chapter 5, Jesus is added to the scene of God on His throne and introduced as "the Lamb who was slain." Let's read it.

REVELATION 5:1-14

1 "I saw, in the right hand of him who sat on the throne, a book written inside and outside, sealed shut with seven seals. 2 I saw a mighty angel proclaiming with a loud voice, "Who is worthy to open the book, and to break its seals?" 3 No one in heaven above, or on the earth, or

under the earth, was able to open the book, or to look in it. ⁴ And I wept much, because no one was found worthy to open the book, or to look in it. ⁵ One of the elders said to me, "Don't weep. Behold, the Lion who is of the tribe of Judah, the Root of David, has overcome; he who opens the book and its seven seals." ⁶ I saw in the middle of the throne and of the four living creatures, and in the middle of the elders, a Lamb standing, as though it had been slain, having seven horns, and seven eyes, which are the seven Spirits of God, sent out into all the earth. ⁷ Then he came, and he took it out of the right hand of him who sat on the throne. ⁸ Now when he had taken the book, the four living creatures and the twenty-four elders fell down before the Lamb, each one having a harp, and golden bowls full of incense, which are the prayers of the saints. ⁹ They sang a new song, saying,

> *"You are worthy to take the book,*
> *and to open its seals:*
> *for you were killed,*
> *and bought us for God with your blood,*
> *out of every tribe, language, people, and nation,*
> *¹⁰ and made us kings and priests to our God,*
> *and we will reign on the earth."*

¹¹ I saw, and I heard something like a voice of many angels around the throne, the living creatures, and the elders; and the number of them was ten thousands of ten thousands, and thousands of thousands; ¹² saying with a loud voice, "Worthy is the Lamb who has been killed to receive the power, wealth, wisdom, strength, honor, glory, and blessing!"

¹³ I heard every created thing which is in heaven, on the earth, under the earth, on the sea, and everything in them, saying, "To him who sits on the throne, and to the Lamb be the blessing, the honor, the glory, and the dominion, forever and ever! Amen!"

14 The four living creatures said, "Amen!" Then the elders fell down and worshiped."

I want you to picture the scene in heaven as John describes it in Chapter 5: God is sitting on the throne. In His hand is a scroll with seven seals and writing on both sides. An angel asks for someone to step forward who is worthy enough to open the scroll, but no one responds because no one can be found worthy enough. John is upset at that, but an elder tells him not to worry, because the Lion of the tribe of Judah and the Root of David is able to open the scroll. John turns and looks, and there he sees not a Lion, but a Lamb. This Lamb looks like he had been slain, but is now fully alive. It's Christ, of course, and He takes the scroll from the hand of God, and at that, all heaven breaks forth into song. The four living creatures and twenty four elders we saw in Chapter four sing about Christ's worthiness because He redeemed mankind back to God. And then millions upon millions of angels sing that famous chorus that we hear in Handel's Messiah, "Worthy is the Lamb who was slain." And then finally, all creation sings praise and honor and glory to the Lamb.

This scene in Chapter 5 is the high point of the book of Revelation. Now, you might think the high point would be the final destruction of Satan, but it isn't. That event comes in Chapter 20, but by then it seems anti-climatic. Satan was already defeated by Christ's death and resurrection. Satan's doom is inevitable. Here in Chapter 5, Jesus receives the power to finish the job he started at the cross precisely because he went to the cross. This celebration

John describes is what all heaven has been waiting for since the time Satan first opposed God's purpose in the world. This is where Christ receives the honor that is His due for going through that terrible ordeal on the cross for us.

This scene details for us the exaltation that the Apostle Paul talked about in his letter to the Philippian church.

> 5 *"Have this in your mind, which was also in Christ Jesus,* 6 *who, existing in the form of God, didn't consider equality with God a thing to be grasped,* 7 *but emptied himself, taking the form of a servant, being made in the likeness of men.* 8 *And being found in human form, he humbled himself, becoming obedient to the point of death, yes, the death of the cross.* 9 *Therefore God also highly exalted him, and gave to him the name which is above every name;* 10 *that at the name of Jesus every knee should bow, of those in heaven, those on earth, and those under the earth,* 11 *and that every tongue should confess that Jesus Christ is Lord, to the glory of God the Father." (Philippians 2:5-11)*

In these six short verses Paul gives us a complete statement about who Jesus is, with many parallels to Revelation Chapter 5.

- Philippians 2:6 says that Jesus is equal to God. In Revelation 5:9-14 Jesus is praised by the angels with all the honor due God alone.

- Philippians 2:8 tells us Jesus gave up the honor due Him as God, and became a man dying on a cross for us out of obedience to the Father's plan. Revelation 5:9

tells us He was slain and with his blood He bought us out of slavery to sin and brought us back to God.

• Philippians 2:9 tells us that God exalted Him to the highest place, and Revelation 5 records that exaltation.

• Philippians 2:10 tells us that every knee shall bow to Jesus in heaven and on earth and under the earth. Revelation 5:13 tells us every creature in heaven and on earth and under the earth, and on the sea as well, sing Jesus' praises. And in Revelation 5:14, the 24 elders fall down and worship Jesus as Lord because of his self-sacrificing obedience. He alone is worthy to receive power and riches and wisdom and strength and honor and glory and praise.

Paul's understanding of the work of Christ in Philippians and John's understanding in Revelation is very much the same. Jesus was God, but he became man and died for our sins. Jesus is Lord at God's command, with the power and majesty that no mere mortal could ever hold.

Let's look now at some of the Old Testament background of Chapter 5. In verse 1 God holds a scroll that's written on both sides and sealed with seven seals. The scroll and its seals figure prominently in Revelation chapters 5-8. Scholars have debated the meaning of this scroll for years. Yet, it's very similar to the scroll that God gave Ezekiel.

9 "When I looked, behold, a hand was stretched out to me; and, behold, a scroll of a book was in it. 10 He spread it before me. It was written within and without; and lamentations, mourning, and woe were written in it." (Ezekiel 2:9-10)

Ezekiel's scroll was filled with warnings of calamities that would happen to the disobedient people of Israel, and we will see that the scroll in Revelation also contains disasters that will fall on unbelievers. Some scholars think the writing on this scroll in Revelation outlines the destiny of the world. But I view the scroll representing God's sovereignty over the history of our world. As part of the honor that God bestows on Jesus, He gives him this scroll, which gives Jesus the authority and power to carry out what's in it. I find this very much like a king giving written orders to his general, or one of us giving the blueprints for our dream house to a contractor. They now have the plans, they now have the authority, and they have the power to carry out the war, or build the house. But not just anyone could receive Revelation's scroll with seven seals, only Jesus is worthy enough, and we'll shortly discover what happens when the seals are broken one by one and the scroll unrolled.

There's a touch of irony in the elder telling John to look at the Lion of Judah and the Root of David. Both of these terms derive from Old Testament passages (Genesis 49:9 and Isaiah 11:1) and they were titles for the powerful Messiah to come in judgment on the enemies of God. Instead, when John looks, he sees only a Lamb that had been slain. He describes the Lamb as having seven horns and seven eyes, which are equated to the seven spirits of God. I take that to mean that the Lamb has the omnipotence, omniscience and omnipresence of God. The horns symbolize power, and the eyes symbolize the ability to see and know everything going on in the world. The number seven indicates the completeness of the Lamb's power (omnipotence) and knowledge (omniscience). Note that the seven Spirits of God are sent out into the <u>whole</u> world, meaning God's spiritual presence is everywhere. We don't have to search for God because He's not just confined to heaven. He's available to all people everywhere. The image of the Messiah as a slain lamb who would die for the sins of the people comes from Isaiah 53:6-9.

> 6 *"All we like sheep have gone astray.*
> *Everyone has turned to his own way;*
> *and Yahweh has laid on him the iniquity of us all.*
>
> 7 *He was oppressed,*
> *yet when he was afflicted he didn't open his mouth.*
> *As a lamb that is led to the slaughter,*
> *and as a sheep that before its shearers is silent,*
> *so he didn't open his mouth.*
> 8 *He was taken away by oppression and judgment;*
> *and as for his generation,*
> *who considered that he was cut off out of the land of the*
> *living and stricken for the disobedience of my people?*
> 9 *They made his grave with the wicked,*
> *and with a rich man in his death;*
> *although he had done no violence,*
> *nor was any deceit in his mouth." (Isaiah 53:6-9)*

After Jesus died, this chapter in Isaiah was instantly recognized as a prediction that the Messiah would die for the sins of the people.

For most Jews, the Messiah was to be a warrior, not a lamb. He was going to be victorious in battle, and not going to suffer and die. They saw victory coming through strength of arms, not in giving yourself away for others. On the other hand, the concept of a Lamb dying to save people was deeply rooted in Jewish history. Passover, for example, is all about lambs being slain so that God's people might live, be redeemed from slavery, and brought out of Egypt to freedom from oppression. For Christians, Jesus is the unique Lamb of God, whose blood was shed to redeem us from our bondage, our enslavement to sin, to bring us back to God. That's what Revelation 5:9 means when it says, "with your blood you purchased men for God." That redemption, or buying back, covers people from every tribe, every language and every nation. Not just the people of Israel are redeemed, but everyone, Jew and Gentile alike, who accepts Jesus as Messiah and Lord.

This is a rich chapter in the Bible: John proclaims the divinity of Jesus in these verses. He explains the nature of Jesus' Messiah-ship as well. We read about our salvation through Jesus' death on the cross. We can see a resurrected and glorified Christ. And we discover whom we should worship and why. There's a timelessness to this scene in heaven. Because John was in the Spirit, it takes place in the time frame of the spiritual world, where all things are present, and there is no past and no future. Jesus is glorified and honored in heaven on the time scale of eternity because of what He did when He was here nearly 2000 years ago in our time scale.

Let's see in the next chapter what happens as Jesus unrolls the scroll breaking each seal one at a time.

OPENING THE FIRST SIX SEALS OF THE SCROLL

I delayed putting some organization to the book of Revelation until this point because I wanted the book to speak for itself. But, beginning with chapter 6, I think some organization will help in understanding the rest of the book. There have been at least five major ways of understanding Revelation throughout history. Each position has been held by devout Christians throughout the ages, and we shouldn't arbitrarily dismiss what other Christians have understood when they read these pages.

The first way of interpreting Revelation is called the Preterist approach, and it says that Revelation is only talking about the times of the early Christians, where Rome is the beast that opposes God, but will be destroyed by the risen Christ. There's a lot to be said for this approach, because it would be easily understood by Christians in the first century. But when Rome was not destroyed by God at that time, Christians then turned to the Allegorical approach, which said that Revelation is all about the spiritual battle between God and Satan rather than about history, and none of the details have much meaning. This was the method of interpreting Revelation used up until the middle ages.

The Reformation led to the Historical approach, which saw Revelation as a prophecy about the actual history of the church through the ages, with the Pope serving as the Antichrist. That fit the revolutionary spirit of the Reformers much better than allegory. This approach, of course, would have had little meaning for the first century Christians. Finally there is the Futurist approach, where the events in Revelation are seen as episodes in the future judgment of God against Satan and unbelievers. There are two sub-groups in the Futurist camp; one sees chapters 1-5 referring to events in the first century, and chapters 6-22 referring to future events. The other group are called Dispensationalists, and they see chapters 1-5 describing the decay of the church over the centuries, with God finally fulfilling His promises to Israel in the Millennium, which sort of merges the Historical approach with the Futurist approach.

Actually, I think valuable insights can be gathered from each of those systems I've outlined. It's my opinion that Revelation defies being organized strictly along the lines of any one approach. After all, it is a series of visions, not a lesson in history. Revelation is apocalyptic which means that it reveals something totally beyond our comprehension. Remember, *apokolypsis* is its name in Greek, meaning "revealing something hidden." It's also prophecy, which means that it's a message to us from God, who sees things from a totally different perspective than we do. And as with most prophecy, the present and the future are intertwined, so that it's often hard to separate what was then from what will be. Take the four horsemen in this chapter of Revelation, for example. Did each of these horsemen represent events current in the lives of first century Christians, or are they symbols of the future? Or are they both? While there are parallels with these horsemen in the prophecies of Zechariah, chapters 1 and 6, in Zechariah the horses are not the harbingers of disaster as they are in Revelation. So we can't really use Zechariah to help us understand these images. We need to look more closely at Revelation chapter 6 itself.

In Revelation chapter 6, note what happens when each of the first six seals of the scroll are opened.

REVELATION 6:1-17

¹ "I saw that the Lamb opened one of the seven seals, and I heard one of the four living creatures saying, as with a voice of thunder, "Come and see!" ² And behold, a white horse, and he who sat on it had a bow. A crown was given to him, and he came out conquering, and to conquer.

³ When he opened the second seal, I heard the second living creature saying, "Come!" ⁴ Another came out, a red horse. To him who sat on it was given power to take peace from the earth, and that they should kill one another. There was given to him a great sword.

⁵ When he opened the third seal, I heard the third living creature saying, "Come and see!" And behold, a black horse, and he who sat on it had a balance in his hand. ⁶ I heard a voice in the middle of the four living creatures saying, "A choenix of wheat for a denarius, and three choenix of barley for a denarius! Don't damage the oil and the wine!"

(Note: A "choenix" in verse 6 is a dry volume measure that is a little more than a liter or quart.)

⁷ When he opened the fourth seal, I heard the fourth living creature saying, "Come and see!" ⁸ And behold, a pale horse, and he who sat on it, his name was Death. Hades followed with him. Authority over one fourth of the earth, to kill with the sword, with famine, with death, and by the wild animals of the earth was given to him.

⁹ When he opened the fifth seal, I saw underneath the altar the souls of those who had been killed for the Word of God, and for the testimony of the Lamb which they had. ¹⁰ They cried with a loud voice, saying, "How long, Master, the holy and true, until you judge and avenge our blood on those who dwell on the earth?" ¹¹ A long white robe was given to each of them. They were told that they should rest yet for a while, until their fellow servants and their brothers, who would also be killed even as they were, should complete their course.

¹² "I saw when he opened the sixth seal, and there was a great earthquake. The sun became black as sackcloth made of hair, and the whole moon became as blood. ¹³ The stars of the sky fell to the earth, like a fig tree dropping its unripe figs when it is shaken by a great wind. ¹⁴ The sky was removed like a scroll when it is rolled up. Every mountain and island were moved out of their places. ¹⁵ The kings of the earth, the princes, the commanding officers, the rich, the strong, and every slave and free person, hid themselves in the caves and in the rocks of the mountains. ¹⁶ They told the mountains and the rocks, "Fall on us, and hide us from the face of him who sits on the throne, and from the wrath of the Lamb, ¹⁷ for the great day of his wrath has come; and who is able to stand?"

Some say the first horseman on the white horse in verse 2 represents Christ, and his riding out to conquer stands for the propagation of the Gospel. But I think it may be more understandable to see this horseman as a parallel to the other horsemen, representing the various powers of destruction that go out to conquer peoples and lands. There were several great empires in the first century: Roman and Parthian, for example. There have been empires in our recent century: English, German, Japanese, Russian, and American. So our first question should be to ask whether the conquering first horseman is from the past, the present, or the future? Or is he more a symbol of man's incessant desire to have power and dominion over others?

The next horseman in verse 4 rides a red horse symbolizing the violence of war with men slaying one another. This isn't limited to the first century, although the Jews in Jerusalem certainly experienced slaughter when the Romans destroyed the city in 70 AD. But, aren't Sudan, Somalia, and Nigeria places where men are slaying each other today for no particular reason? Is this any different than what has happened throughout history? Even as a child I noted that history classes moved from one war to another, as if war was the major milestone of historical change.

The third horseman in black in verse 5 symbolizes scarcity of food with the resulting famine. This could reflect a time when Domitian was emperor in Rome and there was a shortage of grain. Domitian ordered the destruction of half the vineyards to make room for fields of grain, but changed his mind when people threatened to revolt. But, this horseman could also project a future time of scarcity and famine, like we see today in Central Africa or India but even more widespread.

The last horseman in verse 8, the pale rider, death by sword, famine, plague and pestilence, seems to sum up all the devastation of the first three. You may notice that these disasters have historically been caused or spread by human beings. They are not all natural disasters, or calamities that insurance companies would call "Acts of God." Most are the terrible things that we humans do to each other. Are any of these disasters uniquely a sign of the end? Are they something that God has to deliberately set in motion? Is the evil brought about by these four horsemen something new or something old?

It's also possible to view the four horsemen as a sequence that could happen when a future deceiving ruler comes forth portraying himself as a man of peace, but then changes his approach and gains more and more control through waging war. War in turn leads to inflation and the resulting starvation of the poor, which then leads to widespread death. Thus each horseman could represent different stages in the career of the Antichrist, who we'll discuss more in chapter 11.

In the next chapter of Revelation, we will read about a Great Tribulation. Are the calamities in chapter 6 part of that tribulation, or precursors to it? Scholars have debated for centuries whether the Tribulation, a time of incredible oppression and destruction, is behind us or ahead of us, or whether we're in it. In the next chapters, we're going to find that there are worse calamities than the ones mentioned in chapter 6, and it's hard to pick an exact starting or ending point for a measured time of tribulation. That's not surprising: since Revelation is prophecy, time is not necessarily clock time. Things that are described as if they are in sequence may actually be occurring at the same time. So, when the fifth seal is opened, we see martyrs slain for being true to God, who ask, "How long before God brings judgment on all the evil in the world?" This is a question that has no necessary time relationship to the events discussed in the first four seals, or in those to come afterwards. This is a question without time. The martyrs are told in verse 11 that the answer is, "Wait a little more."

As the sixth seal is broken in verse 12, what we would call natural disasters occur: earthquakes, eclipses, and comets. So much so that everyone in the world, from high to low, runs and hides. No one is protected from fear when the earth and the heavens become chaotic and out of control. Earthquakes remind us that we really have no control over nature, and of our insignificance compared to the mountains and marvels like the Grand Canyon. The wonders of nature can bring about awe of God's creation, or it can bring about fear because we're reminded that we're not God, and we're not in control.

STRUCTURE OF REVELATION

I've created a diagram on the next page to help us understand the structure of the rest of the book of Revelation which is often confusing to many readers. So far, we've examined Revelation chapters 1 through 5, read the letters to the seven churches, seen visions of God and Christ, and now looked at the first six seals on the scroll.

Looking at the second line on the chart on the next page, when the seventh seal is finally broken in chapter 8 we are presented with seven trumpets carried by seven angels. But after six of the trumpets have been blown, there's a pause for a little scroll and two witnesses before the seventh trumpet is blown in chapter 11. The seventh trumpet is followed in chapter 16 by seven bowls of wrath that are poured out on earth. Between the seventh trumpet and the first bowl, in chapter 15 there's a rather long sequence that seems to have some connection to what

Structure of Revelation

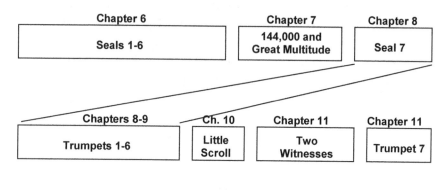

Chapter 1	Chapters 2-3	Chapter 4	Chapter 5
Vision of Christ	Letter to Seven Churches	Vision of God's Throne	Vision of the Scroll and the Lamb

Chapter 6	Chapter 7	Chapter 8
Seals 1-6	144,000 and Great Multitude	Seal 7

Chapters 8-9	Ch. 10	Chapter 11	Chapter 11
Trumpets 1-6	Little Scroll	Two Witnesses	Trumpet 7

Chapters 12-13	Chapter 14	Chapter 14	Chapters 15-16
Dragon & the Two Beasts	144,000	Harvest of Earth	Bowls 1-7

Chapters 17-18	Chapter 19	Chapter 19
Destruction of the Anti-God Political Empire	Armageddon	Destruction of the Anti-Christ and False Prophet

Chapter 20	Chapter 20	Chapter 20
Millennium	Destruction of Satan	Judgment

Chapter 21	Chapter 22
New Heaven and New Earth	Final Instructions to Believers

Copyright 2013, Raymond E. Parry

follows the seventh bowl, involving a dragon, two beasts, 144,000 witnesses and a harvest of Earth. After all the bowls are poured out, there are destructions of political empires, an Antichrist and false prophet, Armageddon, the Millennium, and finally the destruction of Satan in chapter 20 and the creation of a new Heaven and a new Earth in chapter 21. (A millennium merely means one thousand years. The Millennium, or a thousand years of Christ's rule on Earth, is the subject of chapter 20.) And that's what we'll be covering in the rest of the book of Revelation.

A SIMPLER DIAGRAM

But, there's also a simpler top-level diagram of the last days that we can construct based on Jesus' words to his disciples in Matthew chapter 24 the last week in Jerusalem before He was crucified. The first three verses provide the setting, or context, for Jesus' words on the future.

¹ "Jesus went out from the temple, and was going on his way. His disciples came to him to show him the buildings of the temple. ² But he answered them, "You see all of these things, don't you? Most certainly I tell you, there will not be left here one stone on another, that will not be thrown down."

³ As he sat on the Mount of Olives, the disciples came to him privately, saying, "Tell us, when will these things be? What is the sign of your coming, and of the end of the age?" (Matthew 24:1-3)

Here, Jesus and his disciples are leaving the temple grounds and going across the Kidron valley to the Mount of Olives. As they leave, the disciples pointed out the impressive Temple built by King Herod just 50 years before at tremendous expense and labor. Jesus responds to their awe in verse 2, by saying that the temple will be destroyed, with every one of the huge blocks torn down and the building leveled. When they finally reach the Mount of Olives and sit down to rest, the disciples come to Jesus and ask in verse 3, "When will be the destruction of the temple that you prophesied, and what will be the sign of your coming and the end of the age?" They are asking two questions: the first one about the destruction of the Temple they saw as Jesus' unique prophecy with no Old Testament references to explain it; but the second question about the coming of the Messiah and the end of age did have Old Testament references, but nowhere was a time-frame given. Jesus' answers fill the rest of Chapter 24. Look first at Matthew 24:4-8.

> *4 "Jesus answered them, "Be careful that no one leads you astray. 5 For many will come in my name, saying, 'I am the Christ,' and will lead many astray. 6 You will hear of wars and rumors of wars. See that you aren't troubled, for all this must happen, but the end is not yet. 7 For nation will rise against nation, and kingdom against kingdom; and there will be famines, plagues, and earthquakes in various places. 8 But all these things are the beginning of birth pains." (Matthew 24:4-8)*

Wars, famines and earthquakes sound very much like the destruction brought about by the four horsemen of Revelation chapter 6. In verse 8, however, Jesus calls these events "the beginning of the birth pains." He's making a comparison to the onset of labor, with its repeating sharp pains, to say that these early persecutions and oppressions should not be confused with the end of the age. He goes on in Matthew 24:9-14 to say that the persecutions will increase even more, aimed specifically at those who are His followers.

9 "Then they will deliver you up to oppression, and will kill you. You will be hated by all of the nations for my name's sake. 10 Then many will stumble, and will deliver up one another, and will hate one another. 11 Many false prophets will arise, and will lead many astray. 12 Because iniquity will be multiplied, the love of many will grow cold. 13 But he who endures to the end, the same will be saved. 14 This Good News of the Kingdom will be preached in the whole world for a testimony to all the nations, and then the end will come." (Matthew 24:9-14)

Christians will be put to death because of their faith, and hated just because they honor and serve the Lord. In spite of that, in verse 14 Jesus says that the gospel will be preached to the whole world before the end comes. So, if the disciples expected His coming soon, there was a lot of persecution and witnessing yet to be completed. Let's look at what Jesus then says in Matthew 24:15-20.

15 "When, therefore, you see the abomination of desolation, which was spoken of through Daniel the prophet, standing in the holy place (let the reader understand), 16 then let those who are in Judea flee to the mountains. 17 Let him who is on the housetop not go down to take out the things that are in his house. 18 Let him who is in the field not return back to get his clothes. 19 But woe to those who are with child and to nursing mothers in those days! 20 Pray that your flight will not be in the winter, nor on a Sabbath," (Matthew 24:15-20)

To answer their first question about the destruction of the temple, Jesus refers in verse 15 to the prophet Daniel's prediction of an "abomination of desolation" who profanes the temple in Daniel 9:27.

27 "He will make a firm covenant with many for one week. In the middle of the week he will cause the sacrifice and the offering to cease. On the wing of abominations will come one who makes desolate; and even to the full end, and that determined, wrath will be poured out on the desolate." (Daniel 9:27)

Note that the warning to Christians to flee in Matthew 24:15 is given as a "when," not a "then." The destruction of Jerusalem and the temple happens sometime in the midst of the birth pains of verse 8, not necessarily after it. A first "abomination of desolation" happened in 167 BC when Antiochus Epiphanes captured Jerusalem and sacrificed a pig on the altar in the Temple. But the temple was not destroyed at that time. Jesus said, this kind of thing will happen again, with abominable things done in the temple by profane and evil men. The later Rabbis blamed the destruction of the temple in 70 AD on both the Zealots and the Romans. The Zealots were militant Jewish terrorists of the first century who captured the temple in 66 AD and elevated an unworthy man, Phanni, to the High Priesthood, murdering his competition on the sacred temple grounds. The Romans besieged Jerusalem, finally entering its gates and massacring over one million people who had sought sanctuary within its walls. Titus, the Roman general who later became emperor, ordered all the massive stone blocks of the Temple torn down and thrown over the side of the Temple Mount, where many still remain in their tumbled state today. But even that was not a sign of the end of the age, Jesus goes on in Matthew 24:21-31.

21 "for then there will be great oppression, such as has not been from the beginning of the world until now, no, nor ever will be. 22 Unless those days had been shortened, no flesh would have been saved. But for the sake of the chosen ones, those days will be shortened.

23 "Then if any man tells you, 'Behold, here is the Christ,' or, 'There,' don't believe it. 24 For there will arise false christs, and false prophets, and they will show great signs and wonders, so as to lead astray, if possible, even the chosen ones.

25 "Behold, I have told you beforehand. 26 If therefore they tell you, 'Behold, he is in the wilderness,' don't go out; 'Behold, he is in the inner rooms,' don't believe it. 27 For as the lightning flashes from the east, and is seen even to the west, so will be the coming of the Son of Man. 28 For wherever the carcass is, that is where the vultures gather together. 29 But immediately after the oppression of those days, the sun will be darkened, the moon will not give its light, the stars will fall from the sky, and the powers of the heavens will be shaken; 30 and then the sign of the Son of Man will appear in the sky. Then all the tribes of the earth will mourn, and they will see the Son of Man coming on the clouds of the sky with power and great glory. 31 He will send out his angels with a great sound of a trumpet, and they will gather together his chosen ones from the four winds, from one end of the sky to the other." (Matthew 24:21-31)

In verse 21, which starts with a "then" not a "when," Jesus describes a time of great distress like no other ever before, or ever since; in Greek it's called a *thlipsis megalay*, a Great Tribulation. We'll find those same words used in Revelation 7:14 to describe the experience of a group of 144,000 believers in Heaven. In Matt 24:29, the word "oppression" or "distress" is *thlipsis* again. This verse is a quote from the prophet Joel 2:31, and it sounds just like what happens when the sixth seal in Revelation is broken.

> ³¹ *"The sun will be turned into darkness,*
>   *and the moon into blood,*
> *before the great and terrible day of Yahweh*
>   *comes." (Joel 2:31)*

In Matthew 24:30, Jesus says that it's now that the Son of Man comes, which is the sign of the end of the age the disciples asked about. Coming on the clouds in glory refers back to Daniel 7:13, where Daniel saw a vision of the coming of the Son of Man as ruler of an everlasting kingdom.

> ¹³ *"I saw in the night visions, and behold, there came with the clouds of the sky one like a son of man, and he came even to the ancient of days, and they brought him near before him." (Daniel 7:13)*

Now, if we were to diagram Matthew 24 using a very simplified approach, we find first a time of troubles called birth pains by Jesus, then a time of tribulation without equal, and then He comes again, as shown here. The book of Revelation just adds more detail to this general plan.

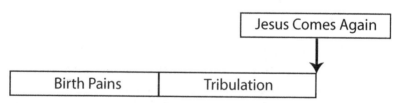

Studying scripture and trying to comprehend how God has planned the destiny of the world is not new, and predicting when the world will come to an end has a long history. In 1555, Nostradamus prophesied in Century 10, Quatrain 72 that,

> "The year 1999, seventh month,
> From the sky will come a great King of Terror:
> To bring back to life the great King of the Mongols,
> Before and after Mars to reign by good luck."

Many took his prophecy to mean the end of the world would arrive in the year 2000. But Nostradamus wasn't the first to see the turning point of the Millennium as an ending point in history, even if his prophecy came to no account. The Talmud in Sanhedrin 97a records a conversation between two rabbis. Rabbi Kattina taught:

> "Six thousand years shall the world exist, and one thousand, the seventh, it shall be desolate, as it is written, 'And the Lord alone shall be exalted in that day.'... Just as the seventh year is one year of release in seven, so is the world: one thousand years out of seven shall be fallow."

To which Rabbi Eliyyahu replied:

> "The world is to exist six thousand years. In the first two thousand there was desolation (because of no Torah); two thousand years the Torah flourished; and the next two thousand years is the Messianic era, but through our many iniquities all these years have been lost."

One could roughly map their discussion to:

4000 BC to 2000 BC: no Torah
2000 BC to 0:   Torah flourishes
0 to 2000 AD: Age of Messiah
2000 AD to 3000 AD: Millennium of Rest

From the first or second century Christian letter of Barnabas, one of the pseudepigraphal letters, (pseudepigraphal means false writing, in other words written in someone else's name) comes another analysis of the ages of history also based on the idea expressed in Psalm 90:4 that a thousand years are like a day in God's time. Barnabas 15:4-5 comments on the Sabbath at the beginning of the Creation.

> "Notice, children, what is the meaning of "He made an end in six days"? He means this: that the Lord will make an end of everything in six thousand years, for a day with him means a thousand years. And he himself is my witness when he says, "Lo, the day of the Lord shall be as a thousand years." So then, children, in six days, that is in six thousand years, everything will be completed. "And he rested on the seventh day." This means, when his Son comes he will destroy the time of the wicked one, and will judge the godless, and will change the sun and the moon and the stars, and then he will truly rest on the seventh day." *(Epistle of Barnabas 15:4-5, Kirsopp-Lake translation, 1912)*

So, Barnabas says the fulfillment of all the events of Revelation comes during the seventh millennium. Doing a quick calculation using Bishop Ussher's chronology of Creation in the year 4004 BC, which was based on adding up the literal lifetimes given in the Old Testament, at this moment we are a little over the 6000th year from Creation, and are entering the seventh millennium, just like the Rabbis Kattina and Eliyahhu said.

Now, before we get all excited and head for the hills to await the Lord's return, remember four things: first, that the previous 6000 year predictions are not from the Bible, but from Jewish and Christian commentators; secondly, Christians have been expecting Christ's return since the day He ascended into heaven; thirdly, our calendars have several years of error built into them — Jesus' birth was set at year 1 by Dionysius Exiguus in the 6th century, and he made a four year error, which would mean we've already been in the seventh millennium for a number of years; and, fourthly, 6000 years is a very short time in view of the eternity of God's perspective, and His time-table may be quite different. My advice is that we shouldn't spend much time trying to figure out exactly when Christ will come again, but live as if it might be at any time. That's because the Bible tells us that God has His own plan, and isn't bound to man's calculation of calendars and time. Jesus also told us in Matthew 24:36 that even he doesn't know when his second coming will occur, but only that it will come when we least expect it, as he said in Matthew 24:42-44.

36 "But no one knows of that day and hour, not even the angels of heaven, but my Father only.

42 Watch therefore, for you don't know in what hour your Lord comes. 43 But know this, that if the master of the house had known in what watch of the night the thief was coming, he would have watched, and would not have allowed his house to be broken into. 44 Therefore also be ready, for in an hour that you don't expect, the Son of Man will come." (Matthew 24:42-44)

Knowing what may happen in the future can have value by taking our focus off our daily struggles to let us know that there's more going on than just our lives and just today. Studying Revelation helps us to understand what's happening in the world, and to put it into perspective. It's very easy to get caught up in the day to day routine, and forget that we are called by God to be His witnesses in this world. In Matthew 24:45-47, Jesus tells us to keep doing the jobs he's told us to do as His servants.

> 45 *"Who then is the faithful and wise servant, whom his lord has set over his household, to give them their food in due season? 46 Blessed is that servant whom his lord finds doing so when he comes. 47 Most certainly I tell you that he will set him over all that he has." (Matthew 24:45-47)*

There's a whole world out there that still needs to hear about Jesus Christ. I often wonder why there's so much emphasis in Jesus' sayings that the time is short, and that He's coming soon, because it's been nearly 2000 years since He died and rose again. Why hasn't He come back already? The answer has always been so that there would be the opportunity for the gospel to spread and for everyone to have the chance to come to faith.

THE ENTIRETY OF THE PEOPLE OF GOD

Chapter 7 is all about people who have come to faith in Jesus Christ. In the last verse of chapter 6, the question is asked, "Who can stand?" in other words, "Who can survive this tribulation?" And chapter 7 answers that question. Remember back in chapters 2 and 3, we saw seven letters addressed to seven churches that encouraged people in those churches to be overcomers — people who when faced with a challenge to their faith, stayed true to God. Chapter 7 is about those people, but it is also about the God who is faithful to His promises, including those He made to the Jewish people. Look at Romans 11:25-27 to see what Paul wrote to the Roman Christians about the ultimate salvation of the Jewish people.

25 "For I don't desire you to be ignorant, brothers, of this mystery, so that you won't be wise in your own conceits, that a partial hardening has happened to Israel, until the fullness of the Gentiles has come in, 26 and so all Israel will be saved. Even as it is written,

> *"There will come out of Zion the Deliverer,*
> *and he will turn away ungodliness from Jacob.*
> *27 This is my covenant with them,*
> *when I will take away their sins." (Romans 11:25-27)*

In these last two sentences, Paul is quoting a conflation of Isaiah 59:20-21 and Isaiah 27:9 to justify his position. In Romans 11:25, Paul summarizes his discussion of chapters 9 to 11, where he's talking about how the Israelites were chosen by God to be His people, but how most of them rejected Jesus as Messiah. As a result, God extended salvation by faith to Gentiles as well. But Paul warned the Gentile Christians not to be conceited. Israel's rejection of Christ is only partial and only temporary. The Gentile opportunity for salvation does not mean that Israel was rejected by God. In Romans 11:1, Paul firmly says "God did not reject his people." He goes on to say in Romans 11:5 that there's always been a remnant in Israel chosen by grace who have kept their faith in God and his Messiah. In Romans 11:25-26, Paul says that after "the full number of Gentiles has come in, all Israel will be saved." Scholars debate as to how many Paul meant by the word "all," but in Revelation 7, we're going to see that John would probably have understood it to mean "Israel as a whole." But before we get there, we need to learn what Paul discovered in Isaiah 59:19-21 concerning the future destiny of the Jewish people.

> *19 "So shall they fear Yahweh's name from the west,*
> *and his glory from the rising of the sun;*
> *for he will come as a rushing stream,*
> *which Yahweh's breath drives.*

> *20 "A Redeemer will come to Zion, and to those who turn from disobedience in Jacob," says Yahweh. 21 "As for me, this is my covenant with them," says Yahweh. "My Spirit who is on you, and my words which I have put in your mouth, shall not depart out of your mouth, nor out of the mouth of your offspring, nor out of the mouth of your*

*offspring's offspring," says Yahweh, "from henceforth
and forever." (Isaiah 59:19-21)*

In this passage from Isaiah, God promises to the
Israelites that the descendants of Israel will be His
witnesses forever. And this promise comes right after
verses filled with God's displeasure with the sins of those
very same Israelites. Verse 2 of Isaiah 59 says their
iniquities have separated them from God, so that He will
not hear them. But in verses 12-13, the Israelites confess
their sins. So, in verse 20, God promises that the Redeemer
will come to those Israelites who repent of their sins. We
can conclude from this discussion in Paul and Isaiah that
the church, made up primarily of Gentiles, does not replace
Israel as God's chosen people, in spite of what some have
taught. Those Jews who repent of their sin of rejecting
Jesus as Savior and Lord <u>will</u> have a role to play as faithful
witnesses to God.

Isaiah 59:19 tells us that from the West and from the
East, people will fear the Lord and revere His glory. It's a
promise that one day, people from one end of the whole
world to the other will come to faith in God. The words
"rising of the sun" or "from the East" translate the Greek
phrase, *ap anatalōn āliou* from the Greek Old Testament,
literally meaning "from the rising of the sun" as the King
James Version translates it. This is the same expression
used in Revelation 7:2 where it says the angel with the seal
of God "ascends from the sunrise" or "ascending from the
East." This is not just a coincidence. When John wrote
Revelation, he alluded to over 280 Old Testament
passages, but he rarely quoted a full verse. The Old
Testament was so familiar to him and to his readers, that a
mere phrase was enough to make them say, "Oh yes, I
know what he's talking about here in Revelation 7:1-8: he's

referring to that great passage in Isaiah 59, where God promises that Israel will be His witnesses forever."

With that background, let's read John's vision of the people of Israel in Revelation 7:1-8.

REVELATION 7:1-8

1 "After this, I saw four angels standing at the four corners of the earth, holding the four winds of the earth, so that no wind would blow on the earth, or on the sea, or on any tree. 2 I saw another angel ascend from the sunrise, having the seal of the living God. He cried with a loud voice to the four angels to whom it was given to harm the earth and the sea, 3 saying, "Don't harm the earth, neither the sea, nor the trees, until we have sealed the bondservants of our God on their foreheads!"

4 I heard the number of those who were sealed, one hundred forty-four thousand, sealed out of every tribe of the children of Israel:

5 of the tribe of Judah were sealed twelve thousand, of the tribe of Reuben twelve thousand, of the tribe of Gad twelve thousand, 6 of the tribe of Asher twelve thousand, of the tribe of Naphtali twelve thousand, of the tribe of Manasseh twelve thousand, 7 of the tribe of Simeon twelve thousand, of the tribe of Levi twelve thousand, of the tribe of Issachar twelve thousand, 8 of the tribe of Zebulun twelve thousand, of the tribe of Joseph twelve thousand, of the tribe of Benjamin were sealed twelve thousand."

This first section of Revelation 7 talks about that great day when Israel will be restored. So when the early

Christians read in Revelation 7:4 that there are 144,000 members of the 12 tribes of Israel sealed by God, they would see the 144,000 as a symbolic number representing all of Israel, and would be reminded of Paul's statement in Romans, that "all Israel will be saved." Revelation confirms that God will be faithful to His promise to Israel in Isaiah 59.

Revelation 7:3 says that these 144,000 Israelites are sealed to protect them from the tribulations about to be unleashed by the angels in verse 1, because their role is to be witnesses for God. In ancient times, winds coming directly from the North, South, East, or West, were seen to be good winds bringing good weather. The winds coming from the angles NE, SE, SW, and NW, which were called the four corners of the earth, were viewed as winds of destruction and violence. These destructive winds will buffet the world during the tribulation, but these 144,000 witnesses are protected by God's seal on their forehead.

Some people question whether the 144,000 people from the 12 tribes represent the Jews, or are they really symbolic of the church. I think they are definitely Jewish people from each of the 12 ancient tribes of Israel, as listed in verses 4-8. Starting in verse 9, however, we read about another great multitude which no one can count, coming from every nation, tribe, people and language.

Let's read Revelation 7:9-17 to see another vast multitude of believers that join in worship along with the angels, elders and the four living creatures.

REVELATION 7:9-17

9 *"After these things I looked, and behold, a great multitude, which no man could count, out of every*

nation and of all tribes, peoples, and languages, standing before the throne and before the Lamb, dressed in white robes, with palm branches in their hands.
¹⁰ They cried with a loud voice, saying, "Salvation be to our God, who sits on the throne, and to the Lamb!"
¹¹ All the angels were standing around the throne, the elders, and the four living creatures; and they fell on their faces before his throne, and worshiped God,
¹² saying, "Amen! Blessing, glory, wisdom, thanksgiving, honor, power, and might, be to our God forever and ever! Amen." ¹³ One of the elders answered, saying to me, "These who are arrayed in the white robes, who are they, and from where did they come?" ¹⁴ I told him, "My lord, you know." He said to me, "These are those who came out of the great tribulation. They washed their robes, and made them white in the Lamb's blood.
¹⁵ Therefore they are before the throne of God, they serve him day and night in his temple. He who sits on the throne will spread his tabernacle over them. ¹⁶ They will never be hungry, neither thirsty any more; neither will the sun beat on them, nor any heat; ¹⁷ for the Lamb who is in the middle of the throne shepherds them, and leads them to springs of life-giving waters. And God will wipe away every tear from their eyes."

The Greek word for nation used in verse 9 is *ethnous* which is the same word we get "ethnic" from. But it's also the same word used for "Gentiles" in Romans 11. There Paul said that the Israelites will return to God when the fullness of the Gentiles is complete, and in verse 9 of Revelation 7, we see that great multitude of Gentiles gathered around the throne. To use Paul's words from Romans 11:25, their "full number" is complete, because they are all here, from every part of the world, every tribe, every nation and every language. Revelation chapter 7 brings together Jewish believers in Christ and Gentile Christians to share in God's eternal Kingdom. The word for "church," by the way, is not used between chapters 3 and 22 of Revelation. Believers in Christ are all part of the Kingdom, whether Jew or Gentile, just as Paul says in Romans 10:12, "There is no distinction between Jew and Gentile; for the same Lord is Lord of all."

What else do we know about the great multitude of Gentiles in verses 9-17? That's the question the elder asked John in verse 13. Who are these people worshipping God from every nationality on earth, and so vast that no one can count them? John doesn't know, so the elder tells him that these are the ones who have come out of the great tribulation. When it says they have washed their robes and made them white in the blood of the Lamb, it means that these are Gentiles who died for their faith in Christ during the tribulation. It may be that they have been converted as a result of the preaching of the 144,000 Israelites.

Both these groups, the 144,000 Israelites and the vast multitude from every nation represent the totality of those who have come to faith in God. They are people who stayed true to their faith, no matter the consequences. Two of the cornerstones in our Christian life are faith in God when we are undergoing trouble, and believing that God will continue to be faithful to us during that trouble. The book of Revelation is full of promises to those who come through tribulation with their faith intact; who don't give up, but are overcomers. To early Christians, Revelation 7 contains many comforting promises that would mean a lot to those going through trouble and persecution. Look at verses 15-17 again. Those who overcome are promised that God will spread His tent over them, which means He lives among them and protects them; that they will never hunger or thirst, nor be scorched by the sun. The Lamb will be their shepherd leading them to springs of living water. And God will wipe away every tear from their eyes. It's a beautiful picture of a life at rest in the arms of God, without struggle or fear or need. That's what heaven is like, and that's the promise to all of us who live in faith through tough times.

STUDY QUESTIONS

Q: How might you describe God to a young child?

Q: What parallels do you see between Philippians 2:6-11 and Revelation 5?

Q: Do you think God causes, or will cause, awful things to happen, or just permits them? Are they because He's angry with us, or because He's trying to get our attention so we'll change?

Q: How does remembering how God has been with you in the past help you through tough times in your life?

SEAL SEVEN AND FOUR
TRUMPETS OF DISASTER

Revelation was a comfort to early Christians even though this chapter and the ones to follow don't seem very hopeful today. In fact, they seem rather scary, because we don't want the disasters prophesied here to happen to us. Maybe we don't even think it sounds like the God we know, the God who loves us. This picture in Revelation seems to be about a totally different kind of God, a God of anger, a God we perhaps find more evident in the Old Testament than in the New. But John's message both here and in his gospel is that God does love us; He loves all of mankind. He sent His son to die for us out of that love, and He's always reaching out to us to bring us back to himself. That's the unifying message of the entire Bible. It's only their total rejection of God that puts people into risk of danger of His wrath. The Bible teaches that there is wrath to come on evil and those who support it. That's what the Day of the Lord is about in the Old and New Testaments; the day when evil will finally be destroyed on this earth, and the Kingdom of God will come in its fullness.

Let's now read Revelation chapter 8 to see what happens when the final seventh seal on the scroll is broken and the first four trumpets of judgment are sounded.

REVELATION 8:1-13

[1] *"When he opened the seventh seal, there was silence in heaven for about half an hour.* [2] *I saw the seven angels who stand before God, and seven trumpets were given to them.* [3] *Another angel came and stood over the altar, having a golden censer. Much incense was given to him, that he should add it to the prayers of all the saints on the golden altar which was before the throne.* [4] *The smoke of the incense, with the prayers of the saints, went up before God out of the angel's hand.* [5] *The angel took the censer, and he filled it with the fire of the altar, and threw it on the earth. Thunders, sounds, lightnings, and an earthquake followed.*

[6] *The seven angels who had the seven trumpets prepared themselves to sound.* [7] *The first sounded, and there followed hail and fire, mixed with blood, and they were thrown to the earth. One third of the earth was burned up,* * *and one third of the trees were burned up, and all green grass was burned up.*

[8] *The second angel sounded, and something like a great burning mountain was thrown into the sea. One third of the sea became blood,* [9] *and one third of the living creatures which were in the sea died. One third of the ships were destroyed.*

[10] *The third angel sounded, and a great star fell from the sky, burning like a torch, and it fell on one third of the rivers, and on the springs of the waters.* [11] *The name of the star is called "Wormwood." One third of the waters became wormwood. Many people died from the waters, because they were made bitter.*

¹² The fourth angel sounded, and one third of the sun was struck, and one third of the moon, and one third of the stars; so that one third of them would be darkened, and the day wouldn't shine for one third of it, and the night in the same way. ¹³ I saw, and I heard an eagle, flying in mid heaven, saying with a loud voice, "Woe! Woe! Woe for those who dwell on the earth, because of the other voices of the trumpets of the three angels, who are yet to sound!"

As soon as the final seal is broken and the scroll is unrolled by the heavenly Christ, there's a half hour of silence as all the worshippers of God in heaven break from their singing and praising to listen to the prayers of the saints ascend before God's throne. I believe the prayers are the prayers of Christians throughout the ages for the coming of Christ at this moment in time, like we find at the end of Paul's first letter to the Corinthians where he says "Maranatha," which means "Come O Lord" in Aramaic. Or prayers like "Come Lord Jesus" that we find at the end of the book of Revelation. And prayers like those of the martyrs we saw in chapter 6, "How long, O Lord, until judgment day when our deaths will be vindicated and the off-balance scales of justice are set right?" For those early Christians who had seen their friends and relatives marched off to execution, their prayer might have been, "How long before good triumphs and evil is destroyed? When will God ring down the final curtain of history?"

Well, Revelation is the vision of how that final curtain might look. We've seen wars and rumors of wars as the first six seals on the scroll were broken, and natural disasters as well, but nothing as severe as we now see when the angels start blowing their trumpets. As each angel blows their trumpet, the disasters seem to get worse and worse, with more and more tribulation for those left on earth. Let's look at the first four trumpets briefly. The first trumpet brings hail and fire mixed with blood that covers about 1/3 of the earth, destroying all the green grass. The second trumpet brings a flaming mass as big as a mountain that falls into the sea, killing 1/3 of the fish and destroying 1/3 of the ships at sea. At the third trumpet, a star named Wormwood falls on 1/3 of the fresh water on the earth, so that people who drink it get sick and die. And the fourth trumpet dims 1/3 of the light of the sun, moon, and stars. Yet the eagle in verse 13 tells us there's even worse yet to come.

What does this mean about God? I think God is trying one last time to get people's attention and make sure that everyone on earth has been brought face to face with the need for faith in Him. God is faithful to us, even when we are not faithful to Him. He fulfills His promises, even when we don't fulfill ours. These terrors and disasters are sent because He loves us, even if we don't love Him. It might seem hard to understand how fire and brimstone come from God's love, but I think that's exactly what it means. You see, we have the tendency to define good and bad on our terms. That's been the case ever since Adam and Eve ate of the tree of the knowledge of good and evil, and discovered they lost God's perspective on things. They started seeing their naked bodies as bad and covered them up, when God had created them that way and pronounced it good. They started lying to God to cover up for what they'd done, when God had created them for open and honest fellowship with Him. When we read Revelation, we tend to label these disasters in Chapter 8 as bad and awful things to have happen, and we miss the point that God is desperately trying to reach people, to make them turn away from their self-centeredness and self-sufficiency, and turn to Him. God always gives people another chance.

Let's take a moment to deal with the subject of God's wrath, how God gets angry with evil. It's not something we like to talk about. We'd rather talk about God's love, how God takes care of us. But we need to talk about both, because in God's way of looking at things, they are connected. Paul says in Romans 1:18 that "the wrath of God is revealed from heaven against all the godlessness and wickedness of men." Evil will be destroyed. Satan isn't in charge, God is. But then Paul goes on to say in Romans 5:9, "since we have been justified by his blood, how much more shall we be saved from God's wrath?"

"Justified" is a legal term, which means we have been found "not guilty." That's the pronouncement of God himself based on our faith in Jesus who died on the cross on our behalf. And "not guilty" means that we are saved from God's wrath by His love. God's love is aimed at His people. God's wrath is aimed at the evil that wants us to not be His people. Remember John 3:16? "For God so loved the world, that he gave his only begotten son, that whosoever believes in him should not perish but have everlasting life." Note that it's God's love that saves us from His wrath. That's good news, because it means that these trials and tribulations we read about here are not aimed at us: they're aimed at people who do not believe in Him, and the whole purpose of them is not to destroy them, but to make them face reality and come to faith. It's like gigantic rumble strips on a country highway. They're there to wake you up because a stop sign or sharp turn is coming. These disasters work the same way as rumble strips, telling people to wake up because the Day of the Lord when God destroys evil from this world is just ahead. You've got one more chance. God wants you to be with Him in the Kingdom of God, and not in the lake of fire with the devil.

The comforting message of Revelation for the early church is that God is going to destroy evil. Evil men will get what they deserve. He's going to balance the scales of justice. People won't be killed anymore for believing in Him. Even though we may think that God is waiting too long to bring an end to our world, the reason is that He's been patient out of love for men and women like you and me. He wants us to come to faith in Him, and He's giving us plenty of opportunity to do that.

Revelation tells us, however, that there will be an end to this present world where good and evil live together in the hearts of men and women. There will be a new world to come where only good will live in our hearts, because God's Kingdom will be totally in place and active. But nowhere in Revelation is there a date set for this time of change. Jesus, in the Gospels, makes that very clear in Matthew 24:36 when He said to His disciples, "No one knows the date or hour, not the angels, not even Me, but only God Himself." The tribulation that we're reading about in Revelation comes not as punishment, but to show unbelievers the reality of life without God, and to bring them to faith. That's why the early church could read these passages and not be afraid of what the future might bring, but instead celebrate the goodness, mercy, patience, and justice of God. If only we could catch but a bit of their boldness, courage, and confidence, what a difference that would make to our lives and to our world.

Two plagues on Unrepentant People

Read Revelation 9 to see what happens as trumpets 5 and 6 are blown, and the reaction of the people to these disasters.

Revelation 9:1-21

¹ "The fifth angel sounded, and I saw a star from the sky which had fallen to the earth. The key to the pit of the abyss was given to him. ² He opened the pit of the abyss, and smoke went up out of the pit, like the smoke from a burning furnace. The sun and the air were darkened because of the smoke from the pit. ³ Then out of the smoke came locusts on the earth, and power was given to them, as the scorpions of the earth have power. ⁴ They were told that they should not hurt the grass of the earth, neither any green thing, neither any tree, but only those people who don't have God's seal on their foreheads. ⁵ They were given power, not to kill them, but to torment them for five months. Their torment was like the torment of a scorpion, when it strikes a person. ⁶ In those days people will seek death, and will in no way find it. They will desire to die, and death will flee from them. ⁷ The shapes of the locusts were like horses prepared for war. On their heads were something like golden crowns, and their faces were like people's faces. ⁸ They had hair like women's hair, and their teeth were like those of lions. ⁹ They had breastplates, like

breastplates of iron. The sound of their wings was like
the sound of chariots, or of many horses rushing to war.
[10] They have tails like those of scorpions, and stings. In
their tails they have power to harm men for five months.
[11] They have over them as king the angel of the abyss. His
name in Hebrew is "Abaddon", but in Greek, he has the
name "Apollyon". [12] The first woe is past. Behold, there
are still two woes coming after this.

[13] The sixth angel sounded. I heard a voice from the
horns of the golden altar which is before God, [14] saying
to the sixth angel who had the trumpet, "Free the four
angels who are bound at the great river Euphrates!"

[15] The four angels were freed who had been prepared for
that hour and day and month and year, so that they
might kill one third of mankind. [16] The number of the
armies of the horsemen was two hundred million. I
heard the number of them. [17] Thus I saw the horses in the
vision, and those who sat on them, having breastplates
of fiery red, hyacinth blue, and sulfur yellow; and the
horses' heads resembled lions' heads. Out of their mouths
proceed fire, smoke, and sulfur. [18] By these three plagues
were one third of mankind killed: by the fire, the smoke,
and the sulfur, which proceeded out of their mouths.
[19] For the power of the horses is in their mouths, and in
their tails. For their tails are like serpents, and have
heads, and with them they harm. [20] The rest of mankind,
who were not killed with these plagues, didn't repent of
the works of their hands, that they wouldn't worship
demons, and the idols of gold, and of silver, and of brass,
and of stone, and of wood; which can't see, hear, or
walk. [21] They didn't repent of their murders, their
sorceries, their sexual immorality, or their thefts."

We need to take note of two things about this particular series of disasters. First, these are disasters brought on mankind by demonic forces, not God's forces; and second, that God allows it to happen. This chapter opens with a star fallen from heaven that has been given the key to the abyss. In the ancient world stars were often seen as spiritual beings. Satan himself is portrayed as a fallen star in Isaiah 14:12 and lightning from heaven in Luke 10:18. However, it's not clear that this star in Revelation 9:1 represents Satan to whom God gives authority to open the doors to this gateway to an evil underworld. It's more likely that this star represents one of God's angels, who is opening the gate of hell to allow the forces of evil to escape to inflict distress on human kind. You might ask, why is God doing this horrible thing? And I think there are two answers to this.

The first is that God wants all people to be saved. He wants all men and women to have a personal relationship with Him, just as Adam and Eve enjoyed in the Garden of Eden before the fall; just as Abraham, Moses, and David enjoyed. But people don't always want to have a relationship with God. The gospel has been widely preached throughout the centuries. Some people have chosen to believe. Others have chosen not to believe.

We all know or have heard about people who came to faith in God after a severe crisis or illness, such as a death of someone close, or a divorce, or a car accident or sickness that puts a person in the hospital, all of which makes them more open to thinking about the meaning of life. If you are in that situation, you might think how out of control life seems, and how vulnerable you are, how easily life is snuffed out, and how suddenly. It's often then that God becomes more real to you, and you are willing to turn your life over to someone stronger than you. Crises are times when people are more open to the gospel, and sometimes God brings crises into your life to get your attention. Not to punish you, but to wake you up and get you to change direction. These tribulations in Revelation are crises like that. They build on each other. They start out as annoyances like the sun and moon being darkened as we saw in chapter 8, then become unpleasant like the bitter water, then painful like the stings of these locusts in the first half of chapter 9, unpleasant enough that people wish for death that never comes. Then finally comes an incredible army of horsemen in the second half of chapter 9 that puts people in real danger of death.

Note in verse 4 that the 144,000 who were sealed by God two chapters ago are not affected by these terrors. Remember also that those who come to faith during this tribulation are the ones we saw in chapter 7 standing in the presence of God. As for the rest of mankind that we read about in verses 20 and 21, those who are not God's selected witnesses, those who have not come to faith, and those who are not killed by the army of 200 million, this remainder does not repent, they do not turn to God and they do not come to faith. Instead, they continue to worship false gods, and continue in lives characterized by stealing, murder, immorality, and sorcery. They had every chance to change their lives to goodness, honesty, faithfulness and love, but turned them all down. Their rejection is not what God wants, but it's basic to the free will that He has given us. Free will comes with consequences. All our choices are not equal, nor free from repercussions. We can choose eternal death rather than eternal life.

When we read about locusts like scorpions, and horses with tails like snakes, we have to remember that

John sees them in a vision, and he keeps trying to explain them as best he can using words that we'll understand. So in verse 7, John tells us the locusts looked like horses; they weren't horses—they *looked* like horses. It's the best analogy John could give us. They wore something like crowns; he couldn't describe it for us exactly, any more than he could what looked like women's hair or lions' teeth. In verse 9 he says the sound of them was like the thundering of many chariots. John uses analogies, and links them to Old Testament passages that his readers could look at and gain understanding. We can find a lot of similarities to this vision in the prophecies of Joel, particularly in Joel 1:1-7, 2:1-5 and 2:12-13.

[1] "Yahweh's word that came to Joel, the son of Pethuel. [2] Hear this, you elders, And listen, all you inhabitants of the land. Has this ever happened in your days, or in the days of your fathers? [3] Tell your children about it, and have your children tell their children, and their children, another generation.

[4] What the swarming locust has left, the great locust has eaten. What the great locust has left, the grasshopper has eaten. What the grasshopper has left, the caterpillar has eaten. [5] Wake up, you drunkards, and weep! Wail, all you drinkers of wine, because of the sweet wine; for it is cut off from your mouth.

[6] For a nation has come up on my land, strong, and without number. His teeth are the teeth of a lion, and he has the fangs of a lioness. [7] He has laid my vine waste, and stripped my fig tree. He has stripped its bark, and thrown it away. Its branches are made white." (Joel 1:1-7)

¹ "Blow the trumpet in Zion,
and sound an alarm in my holy mountain!
Let all the inhabitants of the land tremble,
for the day of Yahweh comes, for it is close at hand:
² A day of darkness and gloominess,
a day of clouds and thick darkness.
As the dawn spreading on the mountains,
a great and strong people;
there has never been the like,
neither will there be any more after them,
even to the years of many generations.
³ A fire devours before them,
and behind them, a flame burns.
The land is as the garden of Eden before them,
and behind them, a desolate wilderness.
Yes, and no one has escaped them.
⁴ Their appearance is as the appearance of horses,
and as horsemen, so do they run.
⁵ Like the noise of chariots on the tops of the mountains
do they leap, like the noise of a flame of fire that devours
the stubble, as a strong people set in battle array." (Joel
2:1-5)

¹² "Yet even now," says Yahweh, "turn to me with all your
heart, and with fasting, and with weeping, and with
mourning."
¹³ Tear your heart, and not your garments,
and turn to Yahweh, your God;
for he is gracious and merciful,
slow to anger, and abundant in loving kindness,
and relents from sending calamity." (Joel 2:12-13)

In Joel 1:4, Joel sees a vision of an army of locusts. In verse 6, he likens the swarm of locusts to an invading nation, which has the teeth of a lion, just like we saw in

Revelation. In Joel 2:1-2, Joel warns the people about the Day of the Lord, which is a day of darkness and destruction, of a mighty army of the locusts. These locusts have the appearance of horses, and in Joel 2:5, we read that they are noisy like chariots. The purpose of destructive army is found in Joel 2:12-13 with a plea for the people to repent and return to the Lord.

In Revelation 9, these locusts come out of the Abyss, which is where God sends angels who have fallen and where demons reside. Remember the man in Luke 8 possessed by a legion of demons and Jesus exorcised them and sent them into the pigs? Where was it they didn't want to go? Luke 8:31 tells us they didn't want to go into the Abyss. In Revelation, the Abyss is where God puts evil spirits and restrains them from doing bad on the earth. In Revelation 9:2, an angel is sent with a key to let them out. So, these locusts are demonic spirits who God has kept under restraint so they can't attack the earth until this point in time: the Day of the Lord that Joel prophesied.

Revelation 9:14 brings us to the second woe, the one that happens when the sixth trumpet is blown. Here we see four angels who have been bound at the Euphrates, and when they are released, their army of 200 million mounted horsemen kills a third of mankind. Because John points out that these angels were bound, or tied up, it indicates that they and their army are not God's angels, but Satan's demonic forces. God has restrained the evil up until this point in time, but now He is allowing evil loose to torment non-believers. They are let loose so that people can see not only how bad evil can be, but how good God has been to keep them locked up. It's almost like God is saying to the world, "So you think worshipping the devil is fun, do you? You think Satanism is harmless? Well, here's a sample of whom you've been worshipping and serving, if that's what it takes to get you to repent." The amazing thing is that even when people are faced with Satan's true intentions which are death and destruction, many would still worship and serve Satan rather than the God who loves them and wants only good for them.

What we see in this chapter of Revelation is that even Satan is limited by God's power. We find in verse 4 that the locusts are not able to harm those sealed by God. In verse 14, the four angels at the Euphrates are bound until God releases them. God's control of evil keeps it from doing its worst. Just imagine if evil forces were never stopped from doing harm. No one would be left alive. Just imagine if we actually got what we deserved, and for every sin there was immediate punishment. Just imagine if for every minor cold or scratch, we'd get a disease that would kill us. That's what would happen if God did not restrain the powers of evil.

This chapter of Revelation was meaningful for Christians in the early church because it told them that God was in control even over the evil forces they saw persecuting them. It also told them that God was a merciful God who wanted even their oppressors to be given the chance to come to faith in Him. It reminded them that the only thing we can do about evil is to repent of our own sin, and spread the gospel of Jesus Christ. But in spite of their efforts to witness to men and women in their world, not everyone was going to be receptive to the Gospel. And so, the final solution to the problem of evil is in God's hands.

10

THE HUGE ANGEL WITH THE LITTLE SCROLL

Review the structure of Revelation chart from chapter 6 showing chapters 4-21 as a series of sevens: seven seals, seven trumpets, and seven bowls. Revelation chapter 10 comes in the interlude between trumpet six and trumpet seven. As each trumpet has sounded, a disaster has come on the earth, and the purpose of the disasters is to get people to repent and turn to God. God is very patient, as you can see in the Bible from beginning to end, as people have come to faith, fallen from faith, come back to faith, fallen away again. God is very patient with us. He's been willing to wait for a long, long time for the world to come back to its Creator. Remember back in chapter 5, the Christians who were martyred for their faith asked God, "How long, O Lord, will you wait?" God replied that they needed to be patient a little longer until all the people who would come to faith have done so.

Read Revelation chapter 10 to hear an angel's instructions to John about what he had seen and heard.

REVELATION 10:1-11

[1] "I saw a mighty angel coming down out of the sky, clothed with a cloud. A rainbow was on his head. His face was like the sun, and his feet like pillars of fire. [2] He had in his hand a little open book. He set his right foot on

the sea, and his left on the land. *3 He cried with a loud voice, as a lion roars. When he cried, the seven thunders uttered their voices. 4 When the seven thunders sounded, I was about to write; but I heard a voice from the sky saying, "Seal up the things which the seven thunders said, and don't write them." 5 The angel whom I saw standing on the sea and on the land lifted up his right hand to the sky, 6 and swore by him who lives forever and ever, who created heaven and the things that are in it, the earth and the things that are in it, and the sea and the things that are in it, that there will no longer be delay, 7 but in the days of the voice of the seventh angel, when he is about to sound, then the mystery of God is finished, as he declared to his servants, the prophets. 8 The voice which I heard from heaven, again speaking with me, said, "Go, take the book which is open in the hand of the angel who stands on the sea and on the land." 9 I went to the angel, telling him to give me the little book. He said to me, "Take it, and eat it up. It will make your stomach bitter, but in your mouth it will be as sweet as honey." 10 I took the little book out of the angel's hand, and ate it up. It was as sweet as honey in my mouth. When I had eaten it, my stomach was made bitter. 11 They told me, "You must prophesy again over many peoples, nations, languages, and kings."*

In verse 6 an angel provides the final answer to the martyrs' question about how long would it be before God takes decisive action by saying, "There will be no more delay." In all these series of seven seals and seven trumpets in Revelation, God has been delaying the Day of Judgment, so that everyone will have a chance to hear the gospel and come to faith. But now, that time is coming to an end. At the end of all the disasters of chapter 9, the ones left behind still refuse to believe in God. For them, verse 7 says the Day of Judgment will come when the seventh trumpet blows. Perhaps that's why whatever the seven thunders say is sealed up; hidden from our sight. There's no need for any more delay before the Day of Judgment.

One of the things that makes interpreting Revelation hard is that John is telling us about visions he had. In these visions he sees people and heavenly beings that have been difficult for him to describe for us. The mighty angel in verse 1 is huge, standing with one foot on the land and the other on the sea. This might be John's figurative way of telling us that this angel has power over the entire earth. The angel holds a little scroll, which John was told to eat. This little scroll would remind readers that Ezekiel in the Old Testament also received a scroll to eat from an angel.

Read Ezekiel 2:9-10 and 3:3-4 to view Ezekiel's experience with eating a scroll provided by an angel.

9 "When I looked, behold, a hand was stretched out to me; and, behold, a scroll of a book was in it. 10 He spread it before me. It was written within and without; and lamentations, mourning, and woe were written in it." (Ezekiel 2:9-10)

3 "He said to me, "Son of man, cause your belly to eat, and fill your bowels with this scroll that I give you." Then I ate it; and it was as sweet as honey in my mouth. 4 He said to me, "Son of man, go to the house of Israel, and speak my words to them." (Ezekiel 3:3-4)

Ezekiel reported that the scroll tasted sweet as honey in his mouth. Eating this scroll led to Ezekiel's call to prophetic ministry, just like Revelation 10:11 tells us about John's renewed call to be a prophet.

But John's scroll in verse 9 is a little different because it's both sweet and sour. Many interpreters focus on the scroll as a literal scroll. Some say it's the same scroll that held the seven seals. Others see it as a summary of the end times. I think this scroll could well be a symbol of what it's like to be God's prophet under oppressive times. The role of prophet can be both sweet and sour at the same time, because while you are preaching salvation to those who will believe, you are also preaching damnation to those who won't believe.

John was told in verse 11 to go again and prophecy once more to peoples, nations, languages and kings. That was his role, whether the message would be sweet or sour to them. His message to the early church was to continue being witnesses to their faith in Jesus Christ in spite of persecution. Don't let your worries or fears distract you from your mission to this world. Don't let the good things of life keep you from your mission either. Don't sit back and say the world is OK as it is, so I don't need to send missionaries or witness or evangelize. Don't say the world is going to hell in a hand-basket, so why bother to send missionaries, or witness or evangelize. And don't be disappointed if your message is rejected. The Christian life contains both sweet and bitter aspects, and no matter what has happened or is happening to us, the job of witnessing and evangelizing is ours as followers of our Lord.

11

TWO WITNESSES AND THE 7TH TRUMPET

Revelation chapter 11 speaks to the problems of living our faith in a world that is anti-God. Many commentators say that chapter 11 is the most difficult chapter to interpret in the whole book of Revelation. But I find the Old Testament helps us understand much of the symbols we find in chapter 11. Let's read Revelation 11:1-14 to learn about two powerful witness for God.

REVELATION 11:1-14

¹ "A reed like a rod was given to me. Someone said, "Rise, and measure God's temple, and the altar, and those who worship in it. ² Leave out the court which is outside of the temple, and don't measure it, for it has been given to the nations. They will tread the holy city under foot for forty-two months. ³ I will give power to my two witnesses, and they will prophesy one thousand two hundred sixty days, clothed in sackcloth." ⁴ These are the two olive trees and the two lamp stands, standing before the Lord of the earth. ⁵ If anyone desires to harm them, fire proceeds out of their mouth and devours their enemies. If anyone desires to harm them, he must be killed in this way. ⁶ These have the power to shut up the sky, that it may not rain during the days of their prophecy. They have power over the waters, to turn them into blood, and to strike the earth with every

*plague, as often as they desire. ⁷ When they have finished
their testimony, the beast that comes up out of the abyss
will make war with them, and overcome them, and kill
them. ⁸ Their dead bodies will be in the street of the great
city, which spiritually is called Sodom and Egypt, where
also their Lord was crucified. ⁹ From among the peoples,
tribes, languages, and nations people will look at their
dead bodies for three and a half days, and will not allow
their dead bodies to be laid in a tomb. ¹⁰ Those who dwell
on the earth rejoice over them, and they will be glad.
They will give gifts to one another, because these two
prophets tormented those who dwell on the earth. ¹¹ After
the three and a half days, the breath of life from God
entered into them, and they stood on their feet. Great
fear fell on those who saw them. ¹² I heard a loud voice
from heaven saying to them, "Come up here!" They went
up into heaven in the cloud, and their enemies saw them.
¹³ In that day there was a great earthquake, and a tenth
of the city fell. Seven thousand people were killed in the
earthquake, and the rest were terrified, and gave glory
to the God of heaven. ¹⁴ The second woe is past. Behold,
the third woe comes quickly."*

The meanings of some of the symbols John uses are
more difficult for us to understand in this day and age than
they would have been to first century Jewish Christians
who had been raised on the Old Testament prophets. Take
measuring the temple, for example. The prophet Ezekiel,
who was held captive in Babylon, reports a vision in
Ezekiel chapter 40 of an angel measuring a new temple in
Jerusalem to replace the one that had been destroyed by
the Babylonians. The reconstruction was finally completed
in a magnificent manner by King Herod. But by John's
time at the end of the first century, that temple had again
been totally destroyed by the Romans. Not a single block

remained. The whole temple mount had been swept clean, and the huge blocks pushed over the side. What makes this chapter difficult to interpret is you first have to decide whether the temple that John mentions is an actual temple rebuilt on Mt. Zion in Jerusalem as some commentators have suggested, or is this temple a symbol for the new people of God as other commentators have proposed? In either case, measuring the temple is seen as God wrapping His protection around God's people within God's temple, while the unbelieving Gentiles or pagan nations trample or destroy the outer court of the temple and the holy city around it.

The 42 lunar months we read about in verse 2 are equal to the 3 1/2 years or 1260 days that we find in verse 3. This time period would remind the first century Christians of Daniel's prophecies of the desecration of the Temple by Antiochus Epiphanes in 167 BC. The feast of Hanukkah is a celebration that 3 and 1/2 years after that desecration, the Maccabees drove Antiochus out and purified the temple. But who are the two witnesses in verse 3? A similar vision that may help explain who they are is found in the prophet Zechariah 4:1-5 and 11-14 with two olive trees representing God's anointed servants.

¹ "The angel who talked with me came again, and wakened me, as a man who is wakened out of his sleep. ² He said to me, "What do you see?" I said, "I have seen, and behold, a lamp stand all of gold, with its bowl on the top of it, and its seven lamps on it; there are seven pipes to each of the lamps, which are on the top of it; ³ and two olive trees by it, one on the right side of the bowl, and the other on the left side of it." ⁴ I answered and spoke to the angel who talked with me, saying, "What are these, my lord?" ⁵ Then the angel who talked with me answered me, "Don't you know what these are?" I said, "No, my lord." (Zechariah 4:1-5)

[11] "Then I asked him, "What are these two olive trees on the right side of the lamp stand and on the left side of it?" [12] I asked him the second time, "What are these two olive branches, which are beside the two golden spouts, that pour the golden oil out of themselves?" [13] He answered me, "Don't you know what these are?" I said, "No, my lord." [14] Then he said, "These are the two anointed ones who stand by the Lord of the whole earth." (Zechariah 4:11-14)

Zechariah had a vision of a golden menorah with an olive tree on either side. He was told by an angel that these two olive trees represented God's anointed servants. For Zechariah, these were Zerubbabel the current ruler, and Joshua, the High Priest at the time Zechariah wrote. Other commentators of Revelation have seen these two witnesses as Moses and Elijah because of verse 6, where they have the power to stop the rain as Elijah did, and to turn water into blood as Moses did. And still other scholars see the two witnesses representing both Jews and Christians as witnesses throughout the centuries to the one true God. I prefer the interpretation that Elijah and Moses are these two witnesses.

John tells us in verse 7 that after the 42 months, the witnesses completed their task, and the beast from the Abyss attacks them and kills them. We first saw the Abyss in chapter 9, out of which came an army of locusts. But there wasn't any mention of a beast in chapters 9 and 10. Visions of fearsome creatures are frequent in the next few chapters. In chapter 13, we will meet another beast that comes up out of the sea, and then one more that comes up out of the land. In chapter 12 we will find a red dragon who appears in heaven, but is cast out to earth, and he is specifically called Satan. I think the beast in verse 7 is one of Satan's servants, possibly the one who's been called the Antichrist, although the name Antichrist is not found in the book of Revelation at all; or the beast may simply represent a country or power like Rome itself, which persecuted believers in God.

John tells us in verse 9 that the bodies of these two witnesses will lie in the streets of the great city for another 3 and 1/2 days, which could represent the 3 and 1/2 years needed to complete a full 7 year period, as in Daniel 9:27. We know that the great city is Jerusalem because he says it's where the Lord was crucified, but he calls Jerusalem Sodom and Egypt because they are the worst names he could think of from the Old Testament. And then God does a miraculous act. He breaths life into their dead bodies, and they stand up, and ascend into heaven, just as Christ did. This is followed by an earthquake that destroys a tenth of the city, and those who survive give glory to God. And then John tells us that the second of the series of three woes announced at the end of chapter 8 is finished.

The main message of this chapter is that if you are faithful witnesses in your life to Jesus Christ, you will be opposed, just like the two witnesses in Chapter 11 were attacked by the beast from the Abyss. Where there is good, Satan will bring evil. Where there is preaching that leads to eternal life, Satan will bring death and destruction. Lest you think life or Revelation ends on a gloomy note, we need to read the rest of Revelation chapter 11.

Let's read Revelation 11:15-19 to be reminded that God is in charge no matter how dark it seems as the seventh trumpet is blown.

REVELATION 11:15-19

15 "The seventh angel sounded, and great voices in heaven followed, saying, "The kingdom of the world has become the Kingdom of our Lord, and of his Christ. He will reign forever and ever!" 16 The twenty-four elders, who sit on their thrones before God's throne, fell on their faces and worshiped God, 17 saying: "We give you thanks, Lord God, the Almighty, the one who is and who was; because you have taken your great power, and reigned. 18 The nations were angry, and your wrath came, as did the time for the dead to be judged, and to give your bondservants the prophets, their reward, as well as to the saints, and those who fear your name, to the small and the great; and to destroy those who destroy the earth." 19 God's temple that is in heaven was opened, and the ark of the Lord's covenant was seen in his temple. Lightnings, sounds, thunders, an earthquake, and great hail followed."

Even John felt that the picture of evil presented in verse 1-14 needed to be balanced by a picture of the glory of God. The second half of verse 15 lets you know that God really is in charge here. If Satan was in any sense the ruler of this world, his kingdom is now God's kingdom. Satan's power has been broken, he's been pushed off the throne, and the Lord will reign for ever and ever.

This is the moment of the last trumpet, the time the Apostle Paul wrote about in I Thessalonians 4:16, "The trumpet shall sound, and the dead shall be raised incorruptible" as we hear in the thrilling piece in Handel's

Messiah. This is the point where the Kingdom of God comes in its fullness. There are yet some details to work out, which will take another 11 chapters of Revelation, but this is the pinnacle moment, known in the Old Testament as the Day of the Lord, and the verses that follow summarize the events to come. The 24 elders around the throne of God in heaven who we first saw in chapter 4 sing a hymn of praise. Verse 17 says that God has finally begun to reign, and in verse 18, we see outlined the final Judgment Day of the Lord. The dead will be judged as to whether they have lived a life of faith in God or not; rewards will be given to God's servants, whom John lists as the prophets, the saints or believers, and those who reverence His name. John includes all believers, great and small. And for those who are not believers, there will be destruction that matches their behavior which tried to destroy the goodness of God's creation.

This chapter would have meant a lot to the early Christians because it let them know that even if they are opposed in their witness, and are killed by forces of evil, God will triumph. He is on the throne, and He does rule over earth and heaven. God will raise these martyrs from death, reward them for their faithfulness, and destroy the powers of evil. In our day, when so many things in the world look gloomy, when people seem uncontrollably bent on destruction, it's good for us to share in the comfort that John gave our fellow Christians nearly 2000 years ago, and to realize that God is in control, and He will win over the forces of evil.

STUDY QUESTIONS

Q: What would be your reaction if there was a knock on your front door, and outside stood a squad of soldiers, and the squad leader said the law requires you to worship the President of the US?

Q: If you were God, when might you have answered the prayers of God's faithful people and rung down the curtain on history? And why might you have waited?

Q: Why doesn't everyone in the world just believe in God and Jesus Christ as Savior and Lord and save themselves from destruction? What are some of the reasons they don't?

Q: Some people say everyone gets into heaven. What would John, who wrote Revelation, say to that?

12

A WOMAN, A DRAGON, AND A BABY

Revelation chapter 12 introduces a woman, a baby, and a dragon. As we read it, we have to continually remind ourselves when we study Revelation, and particularly this chapter, that this book is a series of visions that John saw, and that visions, like our own dreams, are often very symbolic in nature.

REVELATION 12:1-17

¹ "A great sign was seen in heaven: a woman clothed with the sun, and the moon under her feet, and on her head a crown of twelve stars. ² She was with child. She cried out in pain, laboring to give birth. ³ Another sign was seen in heaven. Behold, a great red dragon, having seven heads and ten horns, and on his heads seven crowns. ⁴ His tail drew one third of the stars of the sky, and threw them to the earth. The dragon stood before the woman who was about to give birth, so that when she gave birth he might devour her child. ⁵ She gave birth to a son, a male child, who is to rule all the nations with a rod of iron. Her child was caught up to God, and to his throne. ⁶ The woman fled into the wilderness, where she has a place prepared by God, that there they may nourish her one thousand two hundred sixty days.

⁷ There was war in the sky. Michael and his angels made war on the dragon. The dragon and his angels made war. ⁸ They didn't prevail, neither was a place found for them any more in heaven. ⁹ The great dragon was thrown down, the old serpent, he who is called the devil and Satan, the deceiver of the whole world. He was thrown down to the earth, and his angels were thrown down with him. ¹⁰ I heard a loud voice in heaven, saying, "Now the salvation, the power, and the Kingdom of our God, and the authority of his Christ has come; for the accuser of our brothers has been thrown down, who accuses them before our God day and night. ¹¹ They overcame him because of the Lamb's blood, and because of the word of their testimony. They didn't love their life, even to death. ¹² Therefore rejoice, heavens, and you who dwell in them. Woe to the earth and to the sea, because the devil has gone down to you, having great wrath, knowing that he has but a short time."

¹³ When the dragon saw that he was thrown down to the earth, he persecuted the woman who gave birth to the male child. ¹⁴ Two wings of the great eagle were given to the woman, that she might fly into the wilderness to her place, so that she might be nourished for a time, and times, and half a time, from the face of the serpent. ¹⁵ The serpent spewed water out of his mouth after the woman like a river, that he might cause her to be carried away by the stream. ¹⁶ The earth helped the woman, and the earth opened its mouth and swallowed up the river which the dragon spewed out of his mouth. ¹⁷ The dragon grew angry with the woman, and went away to make war with the rest of her offspring, who keep God's commandments and hold Jesus' testimony."

Chapter 12 feels a lot like a dream that John had, organized as a play with three acts. When you go to a play, quite often you are handed a program that explains what's happening in each act. When we look at Revelation 12, it would be nice to have such a program to help explain what's going on. We can easily figure out the three acts. The first act takes place in heaven and is about a woman who is about to have a baby, and a fierce dragon that wants to destroy the baby. The second act also takes place in heaven, and it's about a war between the dragon, who is now identified as Satan, and God's angels led by the archangel Michael, and Satan loses the war. The third act takes place on earth, and it's about Satan's pursuit after the woman and her offspring.

Some have said the woman is Mary, Jesus' mother, because the male child obviously seems to be Jesus due to the reference to ruling with an iron scepter, which is from Psalm 2:9, a Messianic Psalm.

> 9 *"You shall break them with a rod of iron.*
> *You shall dash them in pieces like a potter's*
> *vessel." (Psalm 2:9)*

Also, this male child is snatched up to God, which could refer to Jesus' resurrection. In John's vision, the woman starts out glorified in Heaven with the signs of the zodiac around her, but ends up in a desert on earth. One problem with identifying the woman as Mary comes in verse 17 where the dragon goes off to make war against all her other offspring, who are all the believers in Christ, which would seem to make them also Mary's physical offspring. Another problem is that the veneration of Mary came much later in history, so first century Christians would not have looked at this picture and automatically seen Mary.

Others have said this woman is Eve, since this chapter is about the conflict between the serpent and her offspring, which reminds us of Genesis 3:15.

15 "I will put hostility between you and the woman, and between your offspring and her offspring. He will bruise your head, and you will bruise his heel." (Genesis 3:15)

If this woman is Eve, then Jesus is one of her descendants, and the other offspring are believers throughout the ages who are also her offspring. Eve then represents the believing part of the human race, which is persecuted by Satan throughout history. The problem with this interpretation is that Eve is not a symbol of belief anywhere in the Bible, but of disobedience.

Another popular interpretation is that the woman represents Israel, which produced Jesus the Messiah, and out of whom came believers whom Satan persecutes. Some commentators view the offspring of Israel as Jewish Christians only. Satan, then, is persecuting Jewish Christians who come to faith during the time of tribulation.

The last interpretation offered by many commentators is that the woman represents the Church, and that the offspring mentioned in verse 17 are believers in the early church who are being persecuted by Satan, and are forced to flee into the desert to escape the destruction of Jerusalem. This interpretation has the problem that the church did not give birth to Jesus. It was the other way around. But in spite of that problem, I prefer this interpretation to the others.

The second act in John's drama starts with verse 7, with a war between the Archangel Michael and his angels on one side and with the dragon and his angels on the other. Verse 9 tells us that the dragon loses the war, and is hurled down to earth along with his angels. The dragon is now identified more specifically as "that ancient serpent, called the devil, or Satan, who deceives the whole world." Throughout the Bible, Satan was originally seen as an angel, who wanted to be equal to God, and was cast out of heaven. The first picture of that fall is seen in Genesis 3:1-5.

1 "Now the serpent was more subtle than any animal of the field which Yahweh God had made. He said to the woman, "Has God really said, 'You shall not eat of any tree of the garden'?" 2 The woman said to the serpent, "We may eat fruit from the trees of the garden, 3 but not the fruit of the tree which is in the middle of the garden. God has said, 'You shall not eat of it. You shall not touch it, lest you die.'" 4 The serpent said to the woman, "You won't really die, 5 for God knows that in the day you eat it, your eyes will be opened, and you will be like God, knowing good and evil." (Genesis 3:1-5)

In the Garden of Eden, Satan is pictured as a serpent who deceives Eve, telling her that if she only eat of the fruit, she would be like God, knowing good and evil. It was only a partial truth, of course. Adam and Eve, who had known only good, now knew about evil, so they began to lie to God. But they certainly did not become like God. If you jump down to verses 14 and 15, you find the punishment that God imposed on the serpent, that it would be cursed, and would be at war with the woman and her offspring.

14 "Yahweh God said to the serpent, "Because you have done this, you are cursed above all livestock, and above every animal of the field. You shall go on your belly and you shall eat dust all the days of your life. ¹⁵ *I will put hostility between you and the woman, and between your offspring and her offspring. He will bruise your head, and you will bruise his heel." (Genesis 3:14-15)*

Revelation pictures this war in Revelation chapter 12, but it began long before in a battle in heaven. Let's read Isaiah 14:12-15, which many view as a picture of Satan's fall from Heaven.

¹² *"How you have fallen from heaven, shining one, son of the dawn! How you are cut down to the ground, who laid the nations low!* ¹³ *You said in your heart, "I will ascend into heaven! I will exalt my throne above the stars of God! I will sit on the mountain of assembly, in the far north!* ¹⁴ *I will ascend above the heights of the clouds! I will make myself like the Most High!"* ¹⁵ *Yet you shall be brought down to Sheol, to the depths of the pit." (Isaiah 14:12-15)*

These verses in Isaiah are part of a taunt against the King of Babylon beginning in Isaiah 14:4. Isaiah charges this person, who other translations call the Morning Star or Lucifer, with trying to raise himself above God and be like the Most High, but instead he is cast down to the depths of the pit, or the Abyss as we find in Revelation. We also can read about this in a Jewish apocalypse written before Jesus' birth, called II Enoch, which was in circulation in the first century. Here are a few verses from II Enoch chapter 29:3-4.

"And one from out the order of angels, having turned away with the order that was under him, conceived an impossible thought, to place his throne higher than the clouds above the earth, that he might become equal in rank to my (God's) power. And I threw him out from the height with his angels, and he was flying in the air continuously above the bottomless (pit)." (II Enoch 29:3-4)

From a different viewpoint, we also can find passages in the Bible that portray Satan as an angel in God's court, where his job is to accuse people of being sinners before God and get them punished as we read in Revelation 12:10. Look at Job 1:6-12 to see Satan portrayed as an accuser of believers.

> [6] *"Now on the day when God's sons came to present themselves before Yahweh, Satan also came among them.* [7] *Yahweh said to Satan, "Where have you come from?" Then Satan answered Yahweh, and said, "From going back and forth in the earth, and from walking up and down in it." [8] Yahweh said to Satan, "Have you considered my servant, Job? For there is no one like him in the earth, a blameless and an upright man, one who fears God, and turns away from evil." [9] Then Satan answered Yahweh, and said, "Does Job fear God for nothing? [10] Haven't you made a hedge around him, and around his house, and around all that he has, on every side? You have blessed the work of his hands, and his substance is increased in the land. [11] But stretch out your hand now, and touch all that he has, and he will renounce you to your face." [12] Yahweh said to Satan, "Behold, all that he has is in your power. Only on himself don't stretch out your hand." So Satan went out from the presence of Yahweh." (Job 1:6-12)*

In this passage in Job, Satan is seen as one of God's angels with a special role to check up on people. He accuses Job before God of believing in God only because God has blessed him, and if his blessings were taken away, Job would curse God instead. One of the other names for Satan is the Devil, which comes from the Greek "*diabolos*," from which we get the words *diablo* and *diabolical*. In Greek, this word means "the slanderer" or "the splitter" or "the accuser." Literally, *diabolos* means to throw something against someone, like a rock or mud or a lie. The Devil said things about Job that were not true to get Job in trouble with God. He also says things about God that aren't true, just as we saw in Genesis. We see a similar story about Satan as an accuser in Zechariah 3:1-2, where Joshua the High priest in Zechariah's day is being judged by an angel of God, and Satan is standing there to accuse him.

¹ "He showed me Joshua the high priest standing before Yahweh's angel, and Satan standing at his right hand to be his adversary. ² Yahweh said to Satan, "Yahweh rebuke you, Satan! Yes, Yahweh who has chosen Jerusalem rebuke you! Isn't this a burning stick plucked out of the fire?" (Zechariah 3:1-2)

In verse 2, we see that Satan is rebuked by God for his accusations. The meaning of the name Satan as "the adversary" or "the accuser" comes from a courtroom setting. Imagine being brought before God for judgment and at the prosecutor's table is Satan, ready to accuse you of all the sins you've ever committed and all the times when you doubted God's presence in your life. But on your side, at the table of the defense, sits your attorney, Jesus. Jesus reminds God how you believed and trusted in Him as Savior and Lord, tried to live as His follower, and how he has already paid the penalty for your sin. And God pronounces the sentence, "Not Guilty."

One of the things I've learned through studying the scriptures is that Satan is not really as big and powerful as he makes himself out to be. He's really a con artist. He has a lot of influence only because people listen to his temptations and believe his lies. We shouldn't underestimate him because he knows our weak spots, and uses them to attack us. But, Satan is not all-powerful; he can be defeated. Michael the Archangel defeats him in battle in Revelation 12:7-9. Traditionally, Michael is the angel charged with protecting the people of Israel from spiritual harm. In the book of Daniel, chapter 12:1-3, an angel tells Daniel that there will be a time of distress, but that the Archangel Michael will protect the believers, those whose names are written in the book, and they will be delivered.

[1] "At that time Michael will stand up, the great prince who stands for the children of your people; and there will be a time of trouble, such as never was since there was a nation even to that same time. At that time your people will be delivered, everyone who is found written in the book. [2] Many of those who sleep in the dust of the earth will awake, some to everlasting life, and some to shame and everlasting contempt. [3] Those who are wise will shine as the brightness of the expanse. Those who turn many to righteousness will shine as the stars forever and ever." (Daniel 12:1-3)

Revelation 12 also tells us how believers can overcome Satan. Look at verse 11. There are three ways Christians have power over Satan. First is the blood of the Lamb. When we believe in Jesus Christ as our Savior and Lord, we have the power of Christ's death that cleanses us from sin. Jesus paid the penalty for our sin when he died on the cross. When Satan accuses us of old sins that we've already asked God to forgive, we can tell him that the price has already been paid, those sins have already been forgiven. The second power Christians have over Satan is the words of their testimony. The word of God is very powerful as a weapon against Satan when he tries to deceive us as he did Adam and Eve. Jesus used verses from Deuteronomy to defeat Satan's temptations in the wilderness in Matthew 4:4, 7, and 10.

The third power that Christians have is that they don't love their lives so much that they are afraid of death. Satan has lied to us about death and made it something to be afraid of. Fear is for those who don't believe in Christ. For them, death is eternity without God, without love, without hope, and it is fearful. But for we who believe, death is just our moving from this earthly existence to a heavenly existence in the presence of God. And that's not scary to think of but wonderful. 2000 years ago, Jesus Christ defeated Satan by his obedience. The early Christians defeated Satan by their faith. If we follow their example, we can defeat him too through the power of God in our lives.

13

TWO BEASTS OPPRESS GOD'S PEOPLE

In Chapter 12, we saw that there was a battle in heaven between a dragon, who was Satan, and God's angels led by Michael the archangel. Satan lost the battle and was thrown out of heaven down to earth. There was a warning given to the inhabitants of earth that the dragon was coming filled with fury, because he knew that his time was short. In verse 17 of chapter 12 we read that the dragon was enraged and went off to make war on Christian believers. So now in chapter 13, we see him standing on the shore of the sea, calling forth helpers in his battle. We'll be introduced to two beasts that assist the dragon in his fight against God.

REVELATION 13:1-18

¹ "Then I stood on the sand of the sea. I saw a beast coming up out of the sea, having ten horns and seven heads. On his horns were ten crowns, and on his heads, blasphemous names. ² The beast which I saw was like a leopard, and his feet were like those of a bear, and his mouth like the mouth of a lion. The dragon gave him his power, his throne, and great authority. ³ One of his heads looked like it had been wounded fatally. His fatal wound was healed, and the whole earth marveled at the beast. ⁴ They worshiped the dragon, because he gave his authority to the beast, and they worshiped the beast, saying, "Who is like the beast? Who is able to make war with him?" ⁵ A mouth speaking great things and blasphemy was given to him. Authority to make war for forty-two months was given to him. ⁶ He opened his mouth for blasphemy against God, to blaspheme his name, and his dwelling, those who dwell in heaven. ⁷ It was given to him to make war with the saints, and to overcome them. Authority over every tribe, people, language, and nation was given to him. ⁸ All who dwell on the earth will worship him, everyone whose name has not been written from the foundation of the world in the book of life of the Lamb who has been killed. ⁹ If anyone has an ear, let him hear. ¹⁰ If anyone is to go into captivity, he will go into captivity. If anyone is to be killed with the sword, he must be killed. Here is the endurance and the faith of the saints.

¹¹ I saw another beast coming up out of the earth. He had two horns like a lamb, and he spoke like a dragon. ¹² He exercises all the authority of the first beast in his presence. He makes the earth and those who dwell in it to worship the first beast, whose fatal wound was healed. ¹³ He performs great signs, even making fire come down out of the sky to the earth in the sight of people. ¹⁴ He deceives my own people who dwell on the earth because of the signs he was granted to do in front of the beast; saying to those who dwell on the earth, that they should make an image to the beast who had the sword wound and lived. ¹⁵ It was given to him to give breath to it, to the image of the beast, that the image of the beast should both speak, and cause as many as wouldn't worship the image of the beast to be killed. ¹⁶ He causes all, the small and the great, the rich and the poor, and the free and the slave, to be given marks on their right hands, or on their foreheads; ¹⁷ and that no

one would be able to buy or to sell, unless he has that mark, which is the name of the beast or the number of his name. [18] Here is wisdom. He who has understanding, let him calculate the number of the beast, for it is the number of a man. His number is six hundred sixty-six."

The first helper is a beast from the sea that we see in verse 1, and the second helper is also a beast that we find in verse 11 coming from the earth. Many commentators have noticed an interesting comparison between the dragon and these two beasts and the Christian doctrine of the Trinity. It's almost as if Satan is setting up an imitation trinity of his own, where Satan, who would like to be equal to God, sets himself up on earth as God. Then Satan sets up the first beast as an imitation of Christ. Look at verse 3. The first beast had a fatal wound, but was healed by Satan's power, just as Christ died on the cross and was resurrected by God. This first beast is commonly called the Antichrist.

The name Antichrist doesn't appear in Revelation at all. In the Bible, the name "Antichrist" only appears in the Letters of I John and II John, so let's read I John 2:18 and 22; I John 4:2 and 3; and then II John 7 to find out more about the Antichrist.

[18] "Little children, these are the end times, and as you heard that the Antichrist is coming, even now many antichrists have arisen. By this we know that it is the final hour. [22] Who is the liar but he who denies that Jesus is the Christ? This is the Antichrist, he who denies the Father and the Son." (I John 2:18, 22)

[2] "By this you know the Spirit of God: every spirit who confesses that Jesus Christ has come in the flesh is of God, [3] and every spirit who doesn't confess that Jesus Christ has come in the flesh is not of God, and this is the

spirit of the Antichrist, of whom you have heard that it comes. Now it is in the world already." (I John 4:2-3)

⁷ *"For many deceivers have gone out into the world, those who don't confess that Jesus Christ came in the flesh. This is the deceiver and the Antichrist." (II John 7)*

The issue John is dealing with in these letters is that some people in the churches were denying that Jesus came in the flesh as the Messiah. This idea came from a spin-off group called Gnostics, which comes from the Greek word for "knowledge," because they claimed they had a special knowledge that wasn't revealed to other Christians. The Gospel of Thomas was one of the books they treasured. In Gnostic belief, Jesus was only divine, and not human. Jesus was not God incarnate in Human flesh. And He did not die on the cross. John's message in his letters is that those who taught that Jesus was only divine, and not human, were anti-Christs — literally, against Christ — because they opposed an essential doctrine of the Christian faith. Without the incarnation, John said, there would be no salvation. Jesus the divine Son of God, was born in human flesh so that he could die on the cross for our sins. Only because of the crucifixion and resurrection of Jesus can we be made right with God, have forgiveness of sins, and enjoy eternal life. Without the incarnation of Jesus as God in human flesh, we would have none of the above. According to the Apostle Paul, faith in the incarnate Jesus who died on the cross breaks the power of sin and death, which is the power Satan holds over us. If we accept the gospel, which means to accept Jesus as our Lord and Savior, we defeat Satan.

As we learned from looking at the letters of I and II John, the Antichrist, as a servant of Satan, will oppose the preaching of Christianity, and will also oppose anything that relates to love, compassion, honesty, and truth. He will also attempt to replace Christ in people's worship and devotion. In Revelation 13:14, we find that the second beast seems to have spiritual powers used to deceive people into worshipping the first beast, in imitation of the power-filled works of the Holy Spirit. So there's now a satanic trinity set up on earth as a substitute for the holy trinity of God.

Let's look in more detail at the first beast. In Revelation 13:1-2, John describes him as having 10 horns and seven heads, but also resembling a leopard, a bear and a lion. To a first century Christian, this description would immediately make them think of Daniel's prophecies of four beasts in Daniel chapter 7:1-8, 11-12, and 15-22.

¹ "In the first year of Belshazzar king of Babylon Daniel had a dream and visions of his head on his bed. Then he wrote the dream and told the sum of the matters.
² Daniel spoke and said, "I saw in my vision by night, and, behold, the four winds of the sky broke out on the great sea. ³ Four great animals came up from the sea, different from one another. ⁴ "The first was like a lion, and had eagle's wings. I watched until its wings were plucked, and it was lifted up from the earth, and made to stand on two feet as a man. A man's heart was given to it. ⁵ "Behold, there was another animal, a second, like a bear. It was raised up on one side, and three ribs were in its mouth between its teeth. They said this to it: 'Arise! Devour much flesh!' ⁶ "After this I saw, and behold, another, like a leopard, which had on its back four wings of a bird. The animal also had four heads; and dominion was given to it. ⁷ "After this I saw in the night visions, and, behold, there was a fourth animal, awesome and powerful, and exceedingly strong. It had great iron

teeth. It devoured and broke in pieces, and stamped the residue with its feet. It was different than all the animals that were before it. It had ten horns. [8] "I considered the horns, and behold, there came up among them another horn, a little one, before which three of the first horns were plucked up by the roots: and behold, in this horn were eyes like the eyes of a man, and a mouth speaking great things." (Daniel 7:1-8)

[11] "I watched at that time because of the voice of the great words which the horn spoke. I watched even until the animal was slain, and its body destroyed, and it was given to be burned with fire. [12] As for the rest of the animals, their dominion was taken away; yet their lives were prolonged for a season and a time. (Daniel 7:11-12)

[15] "As for me, Daniel, my spirit was grieved within my body, and the visions of my head troubled me. [16] I came near to one of those who stood by, and asked him the truth concerning all this. "So he told me, and made me know the interpretation of the things. [17] 'These great animals, which are four, are four kings, who will arise out of the earth. [18] But the saints of the Most High will receive the kingdom, and possess the kingdom forever, even forever and ever.' [19] "Then I desired to know the truth concerning the fourth animal, which was different than all of them, exceedingly terrible, whose teeth were of iron, and its nails of bronze; which devoured, broke in pieces, and stamped the residue with its feet; [20] and concerning the ten horns that were on its head, and the other horn which came up, and before which three fell, even that horn that had eyes, and a mouth that spoke great things, whose look was more stout than its fellows. [21] I saw, and the same horn made war with the saints, and prevailed against them, [22] until the ancient of days

came, and judgment was given to the saints of the Most High, and the time came that the saints possessed the kingdom." (Daniel 7:15-22)

Daniel had a dream, which involved a vision of four beasts, the first like a lion, the second like a bear, the third like a leopard, and the fourth had ten horns, the same characteristics of the first beast in Revelation. In verses 16 and 17, you find that these beasts represent four kingdoms that arise from the earth. The last kingdom in verse 7, the one with 10 horns was the most destructive and oppressive. In verse 8, in the middle of these 10 horns, another one sprang up that displaced three of the 10, and it had a mouth that spoke boastfully. In verses 20-21, Daniel is given the interpretation of this part of his vision. The boastful horn waged war against the saints and was defeating them. Now look again at Revelation 13:5. The first beast was given a mouth to utter proud words, and in verse 7 it says that he made war against the saints and conquered them. In spite of the differences, four beasts in Daniel vs. one beast in Revelation, a horn that speaks and wages war vs. the beast itself speaking and waging war, I think the similarities are so great as to tell us these are basically the same vision seen by two different prophets of God at different times and circumstances. The message is the same. There will arise a power that exalts itself at God's expense, and oppresses people who are true to God. This beast holds political power as we see in verse 7, with authority over every tribe, people, language and nation.

Some scholars have identified the beast as the Roman empire itself. The seven heads may represent the seven major emperors of Rome from Augustus up through Titus, and the 10 horns include those seven plus three minor emperors (Galba, Otho, and Vitellius) that came to power and were quickly replaced in the one year between Nero and Vespasian. See the chart below for the order of the early Roman Emperors. We'll look at the chart again in chapter 17.

The Emperors of Rome	
Augustus	31 BC to 14 AD
Tiberius	14 AD to 37 AD
Caligula	37 AD to 41 AD
Claudius	41 AD to 54 AD
Nero	54 AD to 68 AD
Galba	68 AD to 69 AD
Otho	69 AD
Vitellius	69 AD
Vespasian	69 AD to 79 AD
Titus	79 AD to 81 AD
Domitian	81 AD to 96 AD
Nerva	96 AD to 98 AD
Trajan	98 AD to 117 AD
Hadrian	117 AD to 138 AD

Identifying Rome as the beast would fit John's thinking of Rome as the oppressor of Christians during the reign of Domitian, who sent him to prison on Patmos. But in verse 18, John gives us another clue to the identity of the second beast in the number 666. 100 years after John wrote Revelation, Irenaeus, the bishop of Lyon in France, offered three different suggestions for the meaning of 666, but concluded that none of them were certain, and it would be best to leave the identification to a future time and some greater oppressor of Christians. That hasn't prevented people from trying to guess who John meant. Some scholars see this number 666 as a cryptic reference to a Roman emperor in the first century using a system called Gematria. In those days, the Arabic numbering system that we use today wasn't part of Hebrew, Latin, or Greek, so they used a system of letters standing for numbers. Most of us are familiar with the Roman Numerals scheme using I, V, X, L, C, D and M for 1, 5, 10, 50, 100, 500 and 1000, but there was also a Latin gematria system, matching all the letters of the Latin alphabet (plus a few others) with the numbers 1-9, 10-90, and 100-900.

Using the Greek gematria system shown in the chart below, the name "Jesus" in Greek adds up to 888 if the last letter is the regular sigma. But other names could be found that would add up to 888 as well. There are almost infinite possibilities to reach any particular value, just as there are with 666.

GREEK GEMATRIA

α	1	ι	10	ρ	100
β	2	κ	20	σ	200
γ	3	λ	30	υ	400
δ	4	μ	40	τ	300
ε	5	ν	50	φ	500
F*	6	χ	60	ξ	600
ζ	7	ο	70	ψ	700
η	8	π	80	ω	800
θ	9	ϙ*	90	ϡ*	900

* (obsolete Greek letters digamma, koppa and sampi)

For example, the name of the Roman Emperor Domitian who sent John to Patmos can work out to 666 if you play some games with it. First you have to take his full Latin title, Imperator Caesar Domitianus Augustus Germanicus, and translate it into Greek, Autokrator Kaisar

Dometianos Sebastos Germanikos, and then you have to abbreviate each of his names using commonly used abbreviations that you can find on coins and inscriptions. When you add up the values of those abbreviations, it works out to 666. But that's perhaps a little contrived!

The Hebrew gematria system resembles the Greek system, matching the letters of the Hebrew alphabet to numerical units, tens and hundreds. Many people have proposed that John was referring to the evil emperor Nero, instead of Domitian, since Nero was responsible for killing Peter and Paul and many other Christians as well, and if Revelation had been written in Nero's day, calling him the Antichrist would make some sense. But the only way to get 666 out of Nero is to add the Latin nominative ending "n," as in NERON, add the title Caesar to Nero, to make NERON CAESAR, transliterate it into Hebrew, and then apply the Hebrew gematria system instead of Latin to arrive at 666. It seems a little far-fetched. If Nero had been dead for 30 years when John wrote Revelation, he would be an unlikely candidate for THE Antichrist, even though Nero was certainly AN anti-Christ. It may be the wisest course to take the advice of Irenaeus and wait for a future unveiling of the Antichrist.

The second beast in Revelation 13:11 is subordinate to the first beast. Some commentators think he represents the religious establishment that supports the political power of the first beast. Verse 11 tells us he has two horns like a lamb, but speaks like a dragon. In other words, harmless and defenseless like a lamb, perhaps even looking like Jesus, but his words are cunning and deceptive like the serpent in the Garden of Eden. Verse 12 says he receives authority from the first beast, so the religious hierarchy is subservient to the state. This has happened in modern times in Hitler's Germany, Communist Russia, and China, although there were always Christians who worshipped in secret and outside the power of the state. The second beast then convinces the people on earth to worship the first beast. He does this by performing miracles, as we read in verses 13-15. He builds an image of the first beast, and then gives it the ability to speak. If people don't worship the image, they are killed. This reflects John's time, when Christians who didn't worship the emperor were put in prison or executed. Then the beast puts a mark on everyone, young and old, rich or poor, and only those who had the mark could buy or sell. Slaves were often marked with the owners name in Roman times. But this mark is that number 666, the mark of the beast. Anyone who escaped being marked would then starve to death, or be easy to identify and capture.

There are two messages of warning and hope in Revelation 13 for Christians in the midst of this time of the power of the beast, and we find them in verses 9 and 10. John begins by saying "he who has an ear, let him hear." In other words, listen up. Here's something that not everyone will understand, but if you listen closely, you will understand. Then comes verse 10 about being held captive and killed that sounds so obvious as to be meaningless. But for early Christians, they would remember the prophet Jeremiah's warning to those who turn away from God.

¹ "Then Yahweh said to me, "Though Moses and Samuel stood before me, yet my mind would not be toward this people. Cast them out of my sight, and let them go out! ² It will happen, when they tell you, 'Where shall we go out?' Then you shall tell them, 'Yahweh says:
"Such as are for death, to death;
such as are for the sword, to the sword;

such as are for the famine, to the famine;
and such as are for captivity, to captivity.'" (Jeremiah
15:1-2)

Jeremiah's message came from God to the people who
had turned away from Him, who had become unfaithful;
People who were born into the people of God, but didn't
accept that relationship personally for themselves; people
who were impressed by the might and glory of the
kingdoms and cultures around them, and decided to
worship other gods instead of the one true God. For them,
God's message is plain: "Go away from me! Even if Moses
and Samuel were to come and plead with me, I'm not going
to change my heart." But then if they ask, "Where are we to
go?" The response is to death, the sword, starvation,
captivity — wherever the consequences of your own
betrayal of faith in God lead you. If you turn away from
God and choose the way of the sword, then the sword will
be your reward. If you choose to oppress, then you will be
oppressed. If you choose the way of death, by whatever
means, then you will die.

But this message goes to those who follow the beast.
For those who follow God comes a call for patient
endurance and faithfulness, as we see at the end of verse 10
of Revelation 13. The power of the beast is not ultimate. As
Daniel 7:13-22 tells us, the beast will be overthrown by the
Son of Man who is Jesus the Lord.

13 "I saw in the night visions, and behold, there came
with the clouds of the sky one like a son of man, and he
came even to the ancient of days, and they brought him
near before him. 14 Dominion was given him, and glory,
and a kingdom, that all the peoples, nations, and
languages should serve him. His dominion is an

everlasting dominion, which will not pass away, and his
kingdom that which will not be destroyed." (Daniel
7:13-14)

15 "As for me, Daniel, my spirit was grieved within my
body, and the visions of my head troubled me. 16 I came
near to one of those who stood by, and asked him the
truth concerning all this. "So he told me, and made me
know the interpretation of the things. 17 'These great
animals, which are four, are four kings, who will arise
out of the earth. 18 But the saints of the Most High will
receive the kingdom, and possess the kingdom forever,
even forever and ever.'" (Daniel 7:15-18)

19 "Then I desired to know the truth concerning the
fourth animal, which was different than all of them,
exceedingly terrible, whose teeth were of iron, and its
nails of bronze; which devoured, broke in pieces, and
stamped the residue with its feet; 20 and concerning the
ten horns that were on its head, and the other horn
which came up, and before which three fell, even that
horn that had eyes, and a mouth that spoke great things,
whose look was more stout than its fellows. 21 I saw, and
the same horn made war with the saints, and prevailed
against them, 22 until the ancient of days came, and
judgment was given to the saints of the Most High, and
the time came that the saints possessed the
kingdom." (Daniel 7:19-22)

In Daniel 7:21-22, Daniel concludes his vision by
saying that judgment will come on the beast, and the saints
will inherit the kingdom. And in verse 7:13, Daniel says the
Son of Man will come, and be given all the authority and
power of God, and that his dominion will not pass away
like the dominions of earthly kings, but will last forever.

That is the kingdom we are called to by our faithfulness in the midst of whatever tribulation that comes our way.

14

CHARACTERISTICS OF OVERCOMERS

Chapter 14 can be broken into three sections. We've met the 144,000 in the first section before in chapter 7 as 12,000 from each tribe of Israel, representing the ingathering of all the Jews as believers in Jesus the Messiah. They were sealed by God to protect them from harm during the times of tribulation and oppression by Satan and his helpers that we saw in chapters 8 through 13. In Chapter 13, followers of Satan and his gang are sealed on their forehead with the number of the beast. But, these 144,000 were sealed with the name of God and the Lamb on their foreheads. In chapter 14, we see them not only standing with their Savior, but singing triumphant songs of victory. Let's read Revelation 14:1-5 to see the characteristics of the 144,000 believers.

REVELATION 14:1-5

¹ *"I saw, and behold, the Lamb standing on Mount Zion, and with him a number, one hundred forty-four thousand, having his name, and the name of his Father, written on their foreheads. ² I heard a sound from heaven, like the sound of many waters, and like the sound of a great thunder. The sound which I heard was like that of harpists playing on their harps. ³ They sing a new song before the throne, and before the four living creatures and the elders. No one could learn the song except the one hundred forty-four thousand, those who*

had been redeemed out of the earth. 4 These are those who were not defiled with women, for they are virgins. These are those who follow the Lamb wherever he goes. These were redeemed by Jesus from among men, the first fruits to God and to the Lamb. 5 In their mouth was found no lie, for they are blameless."

John gives us four characteristics of the 144,000 in verses 4 and 5 that are important for getting through times of tribulation. These characteristics are: 1) They are not defiled and are pure. 2) They follow the Lamb wherever he goes. 3) They were purchased from among men and were offered as first-fruits to God and the Lamb. 4) They don't lie and are blameless. We might sum these up in four words: morality, faithfulness, submission, and honesty, and those qualities will help us survive the tough times, too.

The characteristic of morality we find in verse 4, where John tells us that the 144,000 were undefiled. Verse 4b in Greek literally says, "For they are virgins" which means they have kept themselves pure and untouched by the immorality of the world around them. I don't believe that the first part of verse four means that sex in marriage is defiling, because that would ignore what the whole Bible says about sex and marriage. Throughout the Bible, sex is seen as a normal part of the relationship between husband and wife. So, when verse 4 talks about defilement, it means that these 144,000 witnesses have not participated in the culture's immorality because they have vowed to remain celibate.

The second characteristic to help you survive tribulation is faithfulness. John tells us that the 144,000 follow the Lamb wherever he goes. They weren't led astray by the imitation Christ we saw in chapter 13, the Antichrist. They weren't misled by the false preaching and miracles of the second beast who was given spiritual power on earth by Satan. The 144,000 stayed true to Christ, no matter what the consequences, whether being denied food and clothing because they didn't have the mark of the beast on their foreheads; or being persecuted or imprisoned because they refused to worship the image of the beast.

The third characteristic to help you survive hard times is submission to God. One of the age-old problems that plagues us is we want to be in control of our own lives, to be masters of our own destiny. But to overcome the powers and temptations that Satan puts in our way takes more than our own determination; it takes God's power. John reminds us that we were purchased from among men by Jesus' death on the cross, and that we are not our own. The Apostle Paul in his letter to the Roman Christians, chapter 12, verse 1, urges us to offer our bodies as living sacrifices holy and pleasing to God, just as John says that these 144,000 were offered as first-fruits to God and the Lamb. When we surrender the control of our lives to God, we are offering our creator the greatest worship we can give — ourselves.

The fourth characteristic is honesty. John writes that no lie was found in the mouths of the 144,000, they are blameless. One of the marks of a true Christian is that you can believe what he or she says. Jesus said, "Let your yes be yes and your no, no." (Matthew 5:37). In other words, don't confuse people with your response. Don't try to skirt around the issue, so no one knows where you stand. Don't confuse the truth with falsehood, because that's what Satan does.

Let's read the second section of Revelation 14 in verses 6-13 to hear the messages three angels announce to those who believe, to the mighty empire, and to those who refuse to believe in God and worship the beast instead.

REVELATION 14:6-13

6 "I saw an angel flying in mid heaven, having an eternal Good News to proclaim to those who dwell on the earth, and to every nation, tribe, language, and people. 7 He said with a loud voice, "Fear the Lord, and give him glory; for the hour of his judgment has come. Worship him who made the heaven, the earth, the sea, and the springs of waters!"

8 Another, a second angel, followed, saying, "Babylon the great has fallen, which has made all the nations to drink of the wine of the wrath of her sexual immorality."
9 Another angel, a third, followed them, saying with a great voice, "If anyone worships the beast and his image, and receives a mark on his forehead, or on his hand, 10 he also will drink of the wine of the wrath of God, which is prepared unmixed in the cup of his anger. He will be tormented with fire and sulfur in the presence of the holy angels, and in the presence of the Lamb. 11 The smoke of their torment goes up forever and ever. They have no rest day and night, those who worship the beast and his image, and whoever receives the mark of his name. 12 Here is the perseverance of the saints, those who keep the commandments of God, and the faith of Jesus."

13 I heard a voice from heaven saying, "Write, 'Blessed are the dead who die in the Lord from now on.'"

"Yes," says the Spirit, "that they may rest from their labors; for their works follow with them."

For those who listen to the beast and follow him instead of Christ, God's angel has the message that we find in verses 9-11. Judgment day is coming, and what God will be looking for is whose mark do you have on your forehead? In other words, whom do you worship and to whom do you belong? For those who have the mark of the beast, torment awaits. For those who have the mark of God and the Lamb, heaven awaits.

Let's read the third section of Revelation 14 in verses 14-20 to have a foretaste of what the coming judgment will be like.

REVELATION 14:14-20

14 "I looked, and behold, a white cloud; and on the cloud one sitting like a son of man, having on his head a golden crown, and in his hand a sharp sickle. 15 Another angel came out of the temple, crying with a loud voice to him who sat on the cloud, "Send your sickle, and reap; for the hour to reap has come; for the harvest of the earth is ripe!" 16 He who sat on the cloud thrust his sickle on the earth, and the earth was reaped.

17 Another angel came out of the temple which is in heaven. He also had a sharp sickle. 18 Another angel came out from the altar, he who has power over fire, and he called with a great voice to him who had the sharp sickle, saying, "Send your sharp sickle, and gather the clusters of the vine of the earth, for the earth's grapes are fully ripe!" 19 The angel thrust his sickle into the earth, and gathered the vintage of the earth, and threw it into the great wine press of the wrath of God. 20 The wine press was trodden outside of the city, and blood came out of the wine press, even to the bridles of the horses, as far as one thousand six hundred stadia."

In verses 14-16, we see an image of Jesus as the son of man from Daniel 7:13, sitting on the clouds of heaven, and coming in judgment to take home his own. The metaphor used here is one of harvesting grain, and I believe in verse 16, Jesus is harvesting the believers from the earth. In verses 17-20 we have an angel harvesting the non-believers and throwing them into the winepress of God's wrath. This vision is a precursor of what Judgment Day will be like, which finally comes in chapter 20, but before that day comes, John explains God's final wrath on Satan and his followers.

The 144,000 symbolize those who are faithful in the midst of persecution and will stand with Jesus at the last day. They represent those who remain true to God in the hardest of times. In the seven letters to the churches in Asia, John calls Christians in each of them to be overcomers. These 144,000 are among those who overcame. They overcame the threats and powers of Satan. They overcame their own fears and temptations. They survived because they lived moral lives, they followed Jesus without swerving, they submitted themselves to God's control, and they were honest before God and their fellow men. John is calling us to pattern ourselves after their model, to be God's people in a darkening world that needs light and truth, where people need the stability of godly values and ethics and standards. That's our role as Christians.

15

OVERCOMERS SING GOD'S PRAISES

In Revelation chapter 15 we observe the overcomers praising God and then the arrival of seven angels carrying seven final bowls of wrath.

REVELATION 15:1-8

[1] "I saw another great and marvelous sign in the sky: seven angels having the seven last plagues, for in them God's wrath is finished. [2] I saw something like a sea of glass mixed with fire, and those who overcame the beast, his image, and the number of his name, standing on the sea of glass, having harps of God. [3] They sang the song of Moses, the servant of God, and the song of the Lamb, saying, "Great and marvelous are your works, Lord God, the Almighty! Righteous and true are your ways, you King of the nations.
[4] Who wouldn't fear you, Lord,
and glorify your name?
For you only are holy.
For all the nations will come and worship before you.
For your righteous acts have been revealed."

[5] After these things I looked, and the temple of the tabernacle of the testimony in heaven was opened. [6] The seven angels who had the seven plagues came out, clothed with pure, bright linen, and wearing golden

*sashes around their breasts. ⁷ One of the four living
creatures gave to the seven angels seven golden bowls
full of the wrath of God, who lives forever and ever. ⁸ The
temple was filled with smoke from the glory of God, and
from his power. No one was able to enter into the
temple, until the seven plagues of the seven angels would
be finished."*

As this new vision opens, John tells us that the ones
who have been victorious over the beast were given harps
by God with which they then sang a song praising God.
Who are these people? They are the ones who have
overcome the pressures to make life easy for themselves
and worship the beast. In Chapters 2 and 3, John
encouraged each Christian in the seven churches to hang in
there and be overcomers, because they will receive the
promises of God. If you remember:

- The overcomers at Ephesus are promised the right to
  eat of the tree of life from the paradise of God.
- The overcomers at Smyrna are promised that they
  won't be hurt by the second death.
- The overcomers at Pergamum are promised that they
  will eat of the hidden manna of God, the miraculous
  food from heaven that fed the Hebrew slaves during the
  Exodus.
- The overcomers at Thyatira are promised that they will
  receive authority to rule over the nations, the same
  nations that are persecuting them now.
- The overcomers at Sardis are promised that they will
  dressed in white, in other words, in the purity of
  heavenly garments.
- The overcomers at Philadelphia are promised that they
  will be pillars in God's temple.

- The overcomers at Laodicea are promised that they will sit on Jesus' throne with Him.

These are the promises of God to Christians throughout the centuries who come face to face with the temptation to conform to the morals and ethics of society instead of the God-given law of righteousness and love, or are tempted to chase after the almighty dollar instead of following Jesus in a life of service and care for each other, or are tempted to bow at the feet of sophistication instead of God; but overcomers resist and stay true to God and Jesus Christ. They don't necessarily stay alive; it seems to me that by the time we reach chapter 16, there are no believers left on earth, they are all in heaven singing the song of Moses and the Lamb that we see in chapter 15. It's like the songs Moses taught the Hebrew people to celebrate God's power in delivering them from Pharaoh and guiding them safely through the desert to the Holy Land.

Look at what the overcomers in Revelation 15:3-4 say about how God has guided and saved them. They sing that God's deeds are great and marvelous; that He is just and true; that He alone is holy; that His acts are righteous, including acts of punishment for unbelievers. John tells us in verse 7 that he saw seven angels come out of the heavenly temple carrying seven golden bowls filled with the wrath of God. In Chapter 16, these seven bowls will be poured out onto the earth in one last attempt to turn people away from worshipping Satan.

16

ANGELS WITH SEVEN BOWLS OF WRATH

Revelation chapter 16 lists the punishments the seven bowls of wrath pour out on the unbelievers left on earth.

REVELATION 16:1-21

1 "I heard a loud voice out of the temple, saying to the seven angels, "Go and pour out the seven bowls of the wrath of God on the earth!"
2 The first went, and poured out his bowl into the earth, and it became a harmful and evil sore on the people who had the mark of the beast, and who worshiped his image.
3 The second angel poured out his bowl into the sea, and it became blood as of a dead man. Every living thing in the sea died.
4 The third poured out his bowl into the rivers and springs of water, and they became blood. 5 I heard the angel of the waters saying, "You are righteous, who are and who were, O Holy One, because you have judged these things. 6 For they poured out the blood of saints and prophets, and you have given them blood to drink. They deserve this." 7 I heard the altar saying, "Yes, Lord God, the Almighty, true and righteous are your judgments."
8 The fourth poured out his bowl on the sun, and it was given to him to scorch men with fire. 9 People were

scorched with great heat, and people blasphemed the name of God who has the power over these plagues. They didn't repent and give him glory.

¹⁰ The fifth poured out his bowl on the throne of the beast, and his kingdom was darkened. They gnawed their tongues because of the pain, ¹¹ and they blasphemed the God of heaven because of their pains and their sores. They didn't repent of their works.

¹² The sixth poured out his bowl on the great river, the Euphrates. Its water was dried up, that the way might be prepared for the kings that come from the sunrise. ¹³ I saw coming out of the mouth of the dragon, and out of the mouth of the beast, and out of the mouth of the false prophet, three unclean spirits, something like frogs; ¹⁴ for they are spirits of demons, performing signs; which go out to the kings of the whole inhabited earth, to gather them together for the war of that great day of God, the Almighty.

¹⁵ "Behold, I come like a thief. Blessed is he who watches, and keeps his clothes, so that he doesn't walk naked, and they see his shame." ¹⁶ He gathered them together into the place which is called in Hebrew, Megiddo.

¹⁷ The seventh poured out his bowl into the air. A loud voice came out of the temple of heaven, from the throne, saying, "It is done!" ¹⁸ There were lightnings, sounds, and thunders; and there was a great earthquake, such as was not since there were men on the earth, so great an earthquake, so mighty. ¹⁹ The great city was divided into three parts, and the cities of the nations fell. Babylon the great was remembered in the sight of God, to give to her the cup of the wine of the fierceness of his wrath. ²⁰ Every island fled away, and the mountains were not found. ²¹ Great hailstones, about the weight of a talent, came down out of the sky on people. People

blasphemed God because of the plague of the hail, for this plague is exceedingly severe."

I know that many people think that because God is the God of Love that everybody gets to heaven. They wouldn't want to believe in a God who would send anyone to hell. But that image of God is not Biblical. The Bible says that God doesn't want to punish anyone; all He asks for is for us to worship Him and obey Him. If people choose to worship some other god, even Satan, and obey that god, then the Bible tells us that there are consequences for that evil. Let's look at the bowls of wrath.

- First bowl (vs. 2): Sores are placed on those that worshipped the beast.
- Second bowl (vs. 3): The sea turns to blood and all the creatures die.
- Third bowl (vs. 4): Fresh water turns to blood.
- Fourth bowl (vs. 8): The sun scorches people.
- Fifth bowl (vs. 10): Darkness covers the earth (note that the people refuse to repent).
- Sixth bowl (vs. 12): The Euphrates dries up so the kings of the East can attack. As a note, the Romans were deathly afraid of an attack by the Parthians who came from Persia, which was on the other side of the Euphrates. (Also note the gathering for battle at Armageddon, or Har Megiddo, the mountain of Megiddo, which is waged in Chapter 19).
- Seventh bowl (vs. 17): A massive earthquake destroys the great city, which could be either Jerusalem or Rome.

There seems to be a lot of parallels between the bowls of wrath and the seven trumpets back in chapters 8 and 9. There, things were affected only partially, like 1/3 of the creatures of the sea dying, but here it's 100%. There are also a lot of parallels in these chapters to the Exodus. The plagues in chapter 16 are a lot like the plagues sent on Egypt to get Pharaoh to change his mind and let the Hebrew slaves go free. Notice that at the fourth and fifth bowls, no matter how awful the plagues are, people are unwilling to repent of their worship of the beast. Which is just like the hard-hearted Pharaoh who was unwilling to let all his captive laborers go free. God may be angry and wanting to destroy Satan and the Antichrist and all those who believe in them, but even at this point, He is still hoping that people will change their minds.

That's the amazing thing about God's mercy towards sinner. As we've learned before, the purpose of the disasters of the seven seals and seven trumpets was to get people's attention and point them to God, to wake them from their lethargy and complacency and tolerance of evil, and turn them to seeking after good. God sent prophets to them to let people know that they needed to repent. We've seen the two special witnesses who spoke about God, but in the end they were killed by the beast. All along, people have been given the opportunity to believe in God, and from a human perspective, you might wonder why bother? People have had plenty of opportunity to hear about God, many chances to decide they don't want a life filled with lies, cheating, and deception. And even here, in the time of the seven bowls of wrath, when you might think it's all over, there are no more chances, this is the end, God's going to wipe it all out. Even here, people are given the opportunity to turn around, to turn to God. But the sad note is that they don't; instead of worshipping God they curse Him.

The lesson we can learn is that God gives us chances to repent even up to the end of our lives. He doesn't give up on us. It's never too late, no matter what we've done, how badly we've screwed up. Nothing we've done is as bad as what the people in Revelation 16 have done. None of our doubt or lapses of faith comes close to the outright rejection we see written here. And yet God was willing to forgive them and take them back into His loving arms. And that should tell us that He's always willing to forgive us and take us back. That's the most amazing part about God — His truly amazing grace that accepts the worst sinner who repents.

17

THE MYSTERIOUS WOMAN
ON THE BEAST

Many scholars think chapter 17 is the hardest chapter in John's whole letter to understand. In previous chapters, John has described the spiritual aspects of the Antichrist, the beast of chapter 13 as a fallen angel in conflict with the heavenly host. In chapter 17, he now is going to describe Antichrist's political aspects as a mover and shaker of the kingdoms of earth and oppressor of the people of God. Let's read Revelation chapter 17 whose main characters are a woman dressed like royalty and a beast with seven heads and ten horns.

REVELATION 17:1-18

[1] "One of the seven angels who had the seven bowls came and spoke with me, saying, "Come here. I will show you the judgment of the great prostitute who sits on many waters, [2] with whom the kings of the earth committed sexual immorality; and those who dwell in the earth were made drunken with the wine of her sexual immorality." [3] He carried me away in the Spirit into a wilderness. I saw a woman sitting on a scarlet-colored beast, full of blasphemous names, having seven heads and ten horns. [4] The woman was dressed in purple and scarlet, and decked with gold and precious stones and pearls, having in her hand a golden cup full of abominations and the impurities of the sexual

immorality of the earth. [5] And on her forehead a name was written, "MYSTERY, BABYLON THE GREAT, THE MOTHER OF THE PROSTITUTES AND OF THE ABOMINATIONS OF THE EARTH."

[6] I saw the woman drunken with the blood of the saints, and with the blood of the martyrs of Jesus. When I saw her, I wondered with great amazement. [7] The angel said to me, "Why do you wonder? I will tell you the mystery of the woman, and of the beast that carries her, which has the seven heads and the ten horns. [8] The beast that you saw was, and is not; and is about to come up out of the abyss and to go into destruction. Those who dwell on the earth and whose names have not been written in the book of life from the foundation of the world will marvel when they see that the beast was, and is not, and shall be present. [9] Here is the mind that has wisdom. The seven heads are seven mountains on which the woman sits. [10] They are seven kings. Five have fallen, the one is, the other has not yet come. When he comes, he must continue a little while. [11] The beast that was, and is not, is himself also an eighth, and is of the seven; and he goes to destruction.

[12] The ten horns that you saw are ten kings who have received no kingdom as yet, but they receive authority as kings, with the beast, for one hour. [13] These have one mind, and they give their power and authority to the beast. [14] These will war against the Lamb, and the Lamb will overcome them, for he is Lord of lords, and King of kings, and those who are with him are called chosen and faithful." [15] He said to me, "The waters which you saw, where the prostitute sits, are peoples, multitudes, nations, and languages. [16] The ten horns which you saw, and the beast, these will hate the prostitute, will make

her desolate, will strip her naked, will eat her flesh, and will burn her utterly with fire. ¹⁷ For God has put in their hearts to do what he has in mind, to be of one mind, and to give their kingdom to the beast, until the words of God should be accomplished. ¹⁸ The woman whom you saw is the great city, which reigns over the kings of the earth."

The beast we've already seen before in chapter 13, and have called the Antichrist. The woman is called the great prostitute because she commits adultery with all the kings of the earth. In other words, she compromises, works deals, does whatever it takes to win. She is called Babylon the Great and the mother of all the abominations on earth. Now to understand who this figure is, we have to go back into the history of Israel to see what Babylon meant to the Jewish people. If you remember, Moses led the Hebrews out of Egypt 1300 years or so before Christ. After about 300 years of being governed by judges like Gideon, Samson, and Samuel, the people demanded a king, so they could be like every other country. So Saul was chosen to be king, and from Saul came a line of kings that lasted until the year 586 BC when Jerusalem was captured by Nebuchadnezzer, the temple built by Solomon was destroyed, and the elite of Jewish society were carried off to captivity in Babylon.

This captivity in Babylon was not at all like when they were slaves in Egypt, because in Babylon the Jews were only resettled, and allowed to work in trades and business. But the Babylonian captivity was like an earthquake that radically upheaved Jewish self-identity and faith. Before, they had thought that God would protect them forever, because their God was the most powerful god in the world, that they were specially in God's care, would always be a nation, and would always have a king descended from

David on the throne. Now all that was gone. Jerusalem and every fortified city in Palestine were destroyed. Only a few poor farmers were left. The religious and political leaders were far from their homeland and their long cherished beliefs threatened. Formidable challenges to their self-identity and long-held faith arose. Is Marduk the Babylonian god stronger than Yahweh, and that's why they won and we lost? Is the Babylonian way of living with all its corruption better, happier, and more successful than living by our law handed down from Moses? 50 years went by and then the Babylonians were overcome by another king, Cyrus, who decided to let the Jews return to Palestine and rebuild it. Some went back, and we find their story in the books of Nehemiah and Ezra, but most of the Jews stayed in Babylon, or went to places like Egypt, Assyria, or Turkey, where they intermarried and mixed their Jewish faith with the worship of other gods.

But the nation of Israel was never the same again. It never again had an independent kingdom of its own with the wealth and prosperity it had enjoyed under David and Solomon. The Jewish faith had been affected, too, by the assimilation of other religions from the far-off lands that many had gone to. Their whole identity had been changed for the worse by their experience in Babylon. So Babylon became a symbol for all that was wrong in the Jewish experience, for all that was wrong with the world. Let's read sections of Jeremiah chapter 51 to hear the prophecies Jeremiah spoke against Babylon.

¹ "Yahweh says:
"Behold, I will raise up against Babylon,
and against those who dwell in Lebkamai, a destroying
wind. ² I will send to Babylon strangers, who will
winnow her. They will empty her land; for in the day of

trouble they will be against her all around." (Jeremiah 51:1-2)

⁶ "Flee out of the middle of Babylon!
Everyone save his own life!
Don't be cut off in her iniquity;
for it is the time of Yahweh's vengeance.
He will render to her a recompense.
⁷ Babylon has been a golden cup in Yahweh's hand,
who made all the earth drunk.
The nations have drunk of her wine;
therefore the nations have gone mad. (Jeremiah 51:6-7)

¹² "Set up a standard against the walls of Babylon!
Make the watch strong!
Set the watchmen, and prepare the ambushes; for
Yahweh has both purposed and done
that which he spoke concerning the inhabitants of
Babylon.
¹³ You who dwell on many waters, abundant in
treasures, your end has come, the measure of your
covetousness." (Jeremiah 51:12-13)

⁵⁴ "The sound of a cry comes from Babylon,
and of great destruction from the land of the Chaldeans!
⁵⁵ For Yahweh lays Babylon waste,
and destroys out of her the great voice!
Their waves roar like many waters.
The noise of their voice is uttered.
⁵⁶ For the destroyer has come on her, even on Babylon.
Her mighty men are taken.
Their bows are broken in pieces,
for Yahweh is a God of retribution.
He will surely repay." (Jeremiah 51:54-56)

Note in Jeremiah 51:7 the gold cup that makes the whole earth drunk and compare that with Revelation 17:4, and 17:2. Also note Jeremiah 51:13 and compare it with Revelation 17:1, with the common theme of "living by many waters." History tells us that Babylon was damaged by innumerable battles after the time of Cyrus, and by the time of John, it lay deserted and in ruins, which is still the case even today. But Babylon lingered on in people's memory as a symbol of a rich, powerful, and corrupt city that oppressed God's people, even though it had disappeared. "Lebkamai" in verse 1 is a codeword for Chaldea, which was also known as Babylon. In John's time, the equivalent of Babylon was Rome, capital of the richest, most powerful, and most corrupt empire that has ever existed on the face of the earth. This prostitute then, is not Babylon, but Rome herself, who many throughout the Mediterranean area actually worshipped as the goddess Roma. Verse 5 tells us that the title of this woman Babylon the Great is a mystery, but we can decode the mystery that this prostitute called Babylon is actually Rome. Rome is the first century oppressor of the people of faith, and Rome will meet the same doom that destroyed Babylon. We'll see that chapter 18 goes on to detail all the destruction that awaits Rome, the persecutor of Christians, much of which came true hundreds of years later when the Germanic tribes swept down out of the north and destroyed Rome's wealth and power.

Verse 9 tells us that understanding all this calls for a mind with wisdom. In other words, John knew that understanding chapter 17 was not all that easy, even to those in the first century. He goes on to explain the mystery of the beast, by saying that the seven horns represent the seven hills on which the woman sits. The seven hills point to Rome which was famous for being built on seven hills. Then John goes on to say that these horns are also seven kings, five which have fallen, one is, one hasn't come yet, but when he comes will only be around for a little while. And then he mentions an eighth king, who is the beast who once was, and now is not, and yet will come. Scholars have wrestled with this riddle for centuries. Some have tried to map the kings into various empires that controlled the world, such as Alexander the Great's, or the Persian empire. In this scheme, Rome is empire number 6, Alexander's number 5, the Persian empire number 4. And what then is number 7? It is a reborn Roman empire of some future time. Other scholars have tried to map these kings to the emperors of Rome, as we saw in chapter 13, where the first 5 take us from Augustus to Nero; we skip the next three because their reigns were so short, Vespasian becomes number 6, Titus number 7, and Domitian number 8, the beast.

How does Domitian become the beast that once was, now is not, and yet will come? In some ways, Domitian was like Nero, and there was a rumor throughout the empire after Nero committed suicide that he was going to come back to life and lead the Parthian army in an invasion of Rome. It never happened, but people kept seeing Nero's worst traits in their public figures. The Roman historian Juvenal called Domitian a bald-headed Nero, and lost his life for it. Since Nero had sent Peter and Paul to their deaths, as well as a lot of other Christians, and the next emperor after Nero to persecute Christians was Domitian, who sent John to prison, it was perhaps natural for John to see a lot of similarity between the two, and to suggest that the Antichrist was a Nero-like Domitian, resurrected by Satan's power to persecute the people of God, and oppose God's rule on Earth.

The basic issue for John, as it was for Jeremiah, was the oppression felt by the people of God from the political empire of the time. The relationship between church and state has been a thorny issue from long before the church began. In some times and places, church and state have been essentially one, with the same ruler over both. In other times and places, the church has dominated the state, and we can all think of places where the state controls the church. In places like the United States, church and state are officially separate, and what laws have power over the affairs of the church are constantly before the courts.

The Apostle Paul, faced with questions from members of the Roman church about what it meant to be in the world, but not of it, told them in Romans 13:1-2 that everyone should submit to the governing authorities, because they were established by God. Even John understands that God gives governments, even evil governments their authority to rule, when he says in Revelation 17:17 that God has put it into the hearts of the 10 kings to accomplish His purposes in the world. But as history shows, and prophets like Jeremiah and John tell us, God takes away that authority from those who rule wrongly. From John's standpoint, a government that oppresses Christians is evil, and even though God may use them to accomplish His purposes, He will also destroy them for their evil. In verse 14, the 10 kings make war against the Lamb, against Christ, and only Christ can overcome them, because He is King of kings, and Lord of lords.

18

THE FALL OF "BABYLON"

Revelation chapter 18 is an extended dirge concerning the final destruction of Babylon, or Rome as Babylon's successor, or whatever city may succeed Rome in the future as the symbolic capital of the anti-God world. Because these are visions, and the language is allegorical, what John may be describing with the epithet Babylon may turn out not to be a specific city at all, but a form of government supported by the primary kingdoms and powers of the world, whose goal is world-wide domination and oppression of the Christian faith. Let's read Revelation 18 to hear the lament over Babylon's destruction.

REVELATION 18:1-24

1 "After these things, I saw another angel coming down out of the sky, having great authority. The earth was illuminated with his glory. 2 He cried with a mighty voice, saying, "Fallen, fallen is Babylon the great, and she has become a habitation of demons, a prison of every unclean spirit, and a prison of every unclean and hateful bird! 3 For all the nations have drunk of the wine of the wrath of her sexual immorality, the kings of the earth committed sexual immorality with her, and the merchants of the earth grew rich from the abundance of her luxury."

4 I heard another voice from heaven, saying, "Come out of her, my people, that you have no participation in her

sins, and that you don't receive of her plagues, 5 for her
sins have reached to the sky, and God has remembered
her iniquities. 6 Return to her just as she returned, and
repay her double as she did, and according to her works.
In the cup which she mixed, mix to her double. 7 However
much she glorified herself, and grew wanton, so much
give her of torment and mourning. For she says in her
heart, 'I sit a queen, and am no widow, and will in no
way see mourning.' 8 Therefore in one day her plagues
will come: death, mourning, and famine; and she will be
utterly burned with fire; for the Lord God who has
judged her is strong. 9 The kings of the earth, who
committed sexual immorality and lived wantonly with
her, will weep and wail over her, when they look at the
smoke of her burning, 10 standing far away for the fear
of her torment, saying, 'Woe, woe, the great city,
Babylon, the strong city! For your judgment has come in
one hour.'

11 The merchants of the earth weep and mourn over her,
for no one buys their merchandise any more;
12 merchandise of gold, silver, precious stones, pearls,
fine linen, purple, silk, scarlet, all expensive wood, every
vessel of ivory, every vessel made of most precious
wood, and of brass, and iron, and marble; 13 and
cinnamon, incense, perfume, frankincense, wine, olive
oil, fine flour, wheat, sheep, horses, chariots, and
people's bodies and souls. 14 The fruits which your soul
lusted after have been lost to you, and all things that
were dainty and sumptuous have perished from you,
and you will find them no more at all. 15 The merchants
of these things, who were made rich by her, will stand
far away for the fear of her torment, weeping and
mourning; 16 saying, 'Woe, woe, the great city, she who
was dressed in fine linen, purple, and scarlet, and

decked with gold and precious stones and pearls! ¹⁷ *For in an hour such great riches are made desolate.' Every ship master, and everyone who sails anywhere, and mariners, and as many as gain their living by sea, stood far away,* ¹⁸ *and cried out as they looked at the smoke of her burning, saying, 'What is like the great city?'* ¹⁹ *They cast dust on their heads, and cried, weeping and mourning, saying, 'Woe, woe, the great city, in which all who had their ships in the sea were made rich by reason of her great wealth!' For she is made desolate in one hour.*

²⁰ *"Rejoice over her, O heaven, you saints, apostles, and prophets; for God has judged your judgment on her."* ²¹ *A mighty angel took up a stone like a great millstone and cast it into the sea, saying, "Thus with violence will Babylon, the great city, be thrown down, and will be found no more at all.* ²² *The voice of harpists, minstrels, flute players, and trumpeters will be heard no more at all in you. No craftsman, of whatever craft, will be found any more at all in you. The sound of a mill will be heard no more at all in you.* ²³ *The light of a lamp will shine no more at all in you. The voice of the bridegroom and of the bride will be heard no more at all in you; for your merchants were the princes of the earth; for with your sorcery all the nations were deceived.* ²⁴ *In her was found the blood of prophets and of saints, and of all who have been slain on the earth."*

When I was a teen-ager, Russia was often mentioned as a candidate for Babylon. Others offered Rome itself, because it fit the description, too. Some have suggested "the great city" means Jerusalem itself, which is destroyed to make room for the New Jerusalem in Chapter 21. Also when I was a teen-ager, I remember people claiming the

UN fills the role. And still others have suggested that the US could be a candidate for Babylon. But, I'm not sure that any of the above quite make the grade, even though various parallels can be pointed out in each of them to what John described. In chapter 18:1-3, an angel announces the doom of Babylonian-like anti-God power, and in verse 4, believers are called to separate themselves from its evil oppression and resistance to God's will. In verse 8, we read the suggestion that the destruction of this world-wide seat of power will take only one day, with plagues attacking the people, and fire consuming the buildings. In verses 9, 17 and 19, it only takes an hour for the destruction to run its course. This is poetry, which only means that the impact of this judgment is very short in its duration, much like the atomic bombs of WWII destroyed Hiroshima and Nagasaki in seconds. As the people of the world view the sudden destruction, they lament the loss of the centralized power and wealth. The first to lament in verses 9-10 are the kings of the earth who supported it, as they lose the source of their power.

The second group in verses 11-17 to lament the passing of Babylon or Rome, or whatever power passes for them in the future, are the merchants who lose the source of their wealth in trade. When I read the list of trade goods, from gold and silver to articles of wood, ivory, and marble, from spices to oil and flour, from cattle to slaves, I wondered could this really describe Rome of the first century? William Barclay in his Daily Study Bible on Revelation reports that the 2nd century AD Greek orator Aelius Aristides in his *Roman Oration* said,

"Merchandise is brought from every land and sea, everything that every season begets, and every country produces, the products of rivers and lakes, the arts of the

Greeks and the barbarians, so that, if anyone were to wish to see all these things, he would either have to visit the whole inhabited world to see them — or to visit Rome...If there is anything you cannot see at Rome, then it is a thing which does not exist and which never existed." (Barclay, Revelation, pt. 2, pg. 155)

Barclay goes on to list the following Roman excesses. Suetonius the Roman historian said of Caligula that he would bathe in hot or cold perfumed oils, drink pearls of great price dissolved in vinegar, and set before his guests loaves and meats of gold. Nero, he said, never wore the same garment twice. He never made a journey with less than a thousand carriages, with his mules shod with silver. Nero spent $100,000 on roses imported from Egypt to decorate the tables at one banquet. Vitellius, who was emperor for less than a year, spent $20,000,000 on banquets, serving such delicacies as peacocks' brains and nightingales' tongues. In the Talmud tractate Kiddushin, we find written, "Ten measures of wealth came down into the world: Rome received nine, and all the rest of the world, one." Small wonder that the merchants of the world would mourn the passing of their rich market.

The last group to mourn the destruction of the great city are the sailors and ship captains, who depended on the trade of the merchants for their livelihood. With the great consumer of the world's goods gone, where would they derive their income? In verses 23 and 24, John summarizes the reasons for the destruction of this powerful and wealthy empire: First, the personal fortunes of the merchants supplying the city and its ruling classes had brought them the arrogance of power and wealth that flaunted God's rule. Secondly, the political manipulation and mesmerizing power had led the nations of the world to follow its lead into depravity, believing its power would never fail. Rome claimed to be the eternal city, and God's message is that it is not. The third reason for judgment is the blood of the saints — the wanton disregard of the value of life, and the targeting of believers in God for elimination. Those three reasons for destruction are not limited to first century Rome, and in fact are reminiscent of Germany under Hitler, and could easily come to pass again as our world becomes more secular and obsessed with power and wealth.

19

THE VICTORIOUS CHRIST

In Revelation chapter 19, John's focus turns away from the destruction of the evil empire, to the victorious Christ. Let's read it to notice the dramatic change.

REVELATION 19:1-21

¹ "After these things I heard something like a loud voice of a great multitude in heaven, saying, "Hallelujah! Salvation, power, and glory belong to our God: ² for true and righteous are his judgments. For he has judged the great prostitute, who corrupted the earth with her sexual immorality, and he has avenged the blood of his servants at her hand." ³ A second said, "Hallelujah! Her smoke goes up forever and ever." ⁴ The twenty-four elders and the four living creatures fell down and worshiped God who sits on the throne, saying, "Amen! Hallelujah!" ⁵ A voice came from the throne, saying, "Give praise to our God, all you his servants, you who fear him, the small and the great!"

⁶ I heard something like the voice of a great multitude, and like the voice of many waters, and like the voice of mighty thunders, saying, "Hallelujah! For the Lord our God, the Almighty, reigns! ⁷ Let's rejoice and be exceedingly glad, and let's give the glory to him. For the marriage of the Lamb has come, and his wife has made herself ready." ⁸ It was given to her that she would array herself in bright, pure, fine linen: for the fine linen is the righteous acts of the saints. ⁹ He said to me, "Write, 'Blessed are those who are invited to the marriage supper of the Lamb.'" He said to me, "These are true words of God." ¹⁰ I fell down before his feet to worship him. He said to me, "Look! Don't do it! I am a fellow bondservant with you and with your brothers who hold the testimony of Jesus. Worship God, for the testimony of Jesus is the Spirit of Prophecy."

¹¹ I saw the heaven opened, and behold, a white horse, and he who sat on it is called Faithful and True. In righteousness he judges and makes war. ¹² His eyes are a flame of fire, and on his head are many crowns. He has names written and a name written which no one knows but he himself. ¹³ He is clothed in a garment sprinkled with blood. His name is called "The Word of God." ¹⁴ The armies which are in heaven followed him on white horses, clothed in white, pure, fine linen. ¹⁵ Out of his mouth proceeds a sharp, double-edged sword, that with it he should strike the nations. He will rule them with an iron rod. He treads the wine press of the fierceness of the wrath of God, the Almighty. ¹⁶ He has on his garment and on his thigh a name written, "KING OF KINGS, AND LORD OF LORDS."

¹⁷ I saw an angel standing in the sun. He cried with a loud voice, saying to all the birds that fly in the sky, "Come! Be gathered together to the great supper of God,* ¹⁸ that you may eat the flesh of kings, the flesh of captains, the flesh of mighty men, and the flesh of horses and of those who sit on them, and the flesh of all men, both free and slave, small and great." ¹⁹ I saw the beast, and the kings of the earth, and their armies, gathered

together to make war against him who sat on the horse, and against his army. ²⁰ The beast was taken, and with him the false prophet who worked the signs in his sight, with which he deceived those who had received the mark of the beast and those who worshiped his image. These two were thrown alive into the lake of fire that burns with sulfur. ²¹ The rest were killed with the sword of him who sat on the horse, the sword which came out of his mouth. All the birds were filled with their flesh."

In Chapter 19 of Revelation we see two entirely different pictures of Christ. The first picture is that of a bridegroom at a wedding. The second picture is that of the Militant Messiah come in judgment on evil. These two pictures, of a bridegroom in heaven celebrating the arrival of his spouse, and that of an avenging and destroying conqueror on earth, may seem incompatible, but they're not. They both come out of the expectations and hopes of the Jewish people that you find recorded in the OT. Let's look at the wedding feast first in Revelation 19:6-9.

The picture John shows us in heaven is of a wedding with a handsome Bridegroom, the Lamb, and his spotless bride. John explains to us that her wedding dress is of fine linen, which he specifically says is bright and clean, representing the righteous acts of the saints. It's a dress of holiness and purity based on the faithful lives of all the believers in God throughout the centuries. In other words, this bride is not some heavenly young woman who will be the consort of a god, as you might find in some ancient Babylonian religion. No, this bride is the church itself, the collection of all the believers in God.

We see that same image in the prophet Hosea, who lived in the eighth century BC. His main message to the

Jewish people was one of rebuke for straying away from
God to worship other gods. In fact, in Hosea 1:9, he
conveys a word from God that because of their sins, they
are no longer God's people and He is no longer their God.
But then Hosea follows that rebuke with a promise that if
they repent and return to the worship of God, that they will
again become God's people, and He will become not only
their God, but their husband. Read Hosea 2:16-23 to hear
God's promise of a new day.

*16 "It will be in that day," says Yahweh,
"that you will call me 'my husband,'
and no longer call me 'my master.'
17 For I will take away the names of the Baals out of her
mouth, and they will no longer be mentioned by name.
18 In that day I will make a covenant for them with the
animals of the field, and with the birds of the sky,
and with the creeping things of the ground.
I will break the bow, the sword, and the battle out of the
land, and will make them lie down safely.
19 I will betroth you to me forever.
Yes, I will betroth you to me in righteousness, in justice,
in loving kindness, and in compassion.
20 I will even betroth you to me in faithfulness;
and you shall know Yahweh.
21 It will happen in that day, I will respond," says
Yahweh, "I will respond to the heavens,
and they will respond to the earth;
22 and the earth will respond to the grain, and the new
wine, and the oil; and they will respond to Jezreel.
23 I will sow her to me in the earth; and I will have mercy
on her who had not obtained mercy;
and I will tell those who were not my people, 'You are
my people;' and they will say, 'My God!'" (Hosea
2:16-23)*

"In that day" Hosea begins, which in the Old Testament always refers to the promised Day of the Lord. That was the day when God's Messiah would come to bring judgment on the evil of the world, and as Isaiah said in Isaiah 65:25, the "wolf and the lamb will feed together and the lion will eat straw like the ox," and in Isaiah 2:4 that nations "will beat their swords into plowshares and their spears into pruning hooks; Nation will not take up sword against nation, nor will they train for war anymore."

"That Day" is a day of peace and celebration that fulfills the hopes of all people. In that day, the true believers in God will call the Lord, "my husband." God will betroth us to Himself in righteousness, justice, love, compassion and faithfulness. Vows will be said that you can see in Hosea 2:23b. Where God once called them "Not my people," He will vow that "You are my people." And we will respond back, "You are my God."

The wedding supper that we see in Revelation 19:9, to which all believers are invited, is the heavenly feast promised throughout the Bible. Read Isaiah 25:6-9 to hear the promise of a feast that God prepares for His people.

6 "In this mountain, Yahweh of Armies will make all peoples a feast of choice meat, a feast of choice wines, of choice meat full of marrow, of well refined choice wines. 7 He will destroy in this mountain the surface of the covering that covers all peoples, and the veil that is spread over all nations. 8 He has swallowed up death forever! The Lord Yahweh will wipe away tears from off all faces. He will take the reproach of his people away from off all the earth, for Yahweh has spoken it. 9 It shall be said in that day, "Behold, this is our God! We have waited for him, and he will save us! This is

Yahweh! We have waited for him. We will be glad and rejoice in his salvation!" (Isaiah 25:6-9)

The promise is that in that day, believers in God from all generations will sit down for a feast prepared by God for his people. He will swallow up death forever, and wipe away all our tears. If we have felt any disgrace in being known as God's people, or called religious radicals, or termed Jesus freaks, that disgrace will be removed, because we will be honored guests at this banquet in heaven. Jesus in Matthew 8:11 said that "many will come from the east and the west to take their place at the feast with Abraham, Isaac and Jacob in the kingdom of heaven." This is a feast of celebration, because God has won, and evil has lost. War is banished, and peace has come. Hate is gone, and love reigns.

This peace and harmony seems quite a contrast to the next section in Revelation 19. Verses 11-21 present a scene of violence and destruction as the Word of God, Jesus the Messiah, goes to war against evil and defeats the Antichrist and all his followers. We've seen the preparation for this great war in the last three chapters, as the Antichrist gathered all the kings of the earth at Armageddon to do battle with God's heavenly army. This section sounds very gruesome as people are killed and their bodies eaten by birds. This is a radically different feast in contrast to the feast in heaven. It is parallel to the description in Ezekiel of the aftermath of the battle between God's forces and the troops of Gog, of the land of Magog. Read Ezekiel 39:11-13, 17-20 to see another description of the aftermath of this battle.

[11] "It will happen in that day, that I will give to Gog a place for burial in Israel, the valley of those who pass

through on the east of the sea; and it will stop those who pass through. They will bury Gog and all his multitude there; and they will call it 'The valley of Hamon Gog'. ¹² The house of Israel will be burying them for seven months, that they may cleanse the land. ¹³ Yes, all the people of the land will bury them; and they will become famous in the day that I will be glorified," says the Lord Yahweh. (Ezekiel 39:11-13)

¹⁷ "You, son of man, thus says the Lord Yahweh: 'Speak to the birds of every sort, and to every animal of the field, "Assemble yourselves, and come; gather yourselves on every side to my sacrifice that I sacrifice for you, even a great sacrifice on the mountains of Israel, that you may eat meat and drink blood. ¹⁸ You shall eat the flesh of the mighty, and drink the blood of the princes of the earth, of rams, of lambs, and of goats, of bulls, all of them fatlings of Bashan. ¹⁹ You shall eat fat until you are full, and drink blood until you are drunk, of my sacrifice which I have sacrificed for you. ²⁰ You shall be filled at my table with horses and chariots, with mighty men, and with all men of war,' says the Lord Yahweh." (Ezekiel 39:17-20)

For many people, this description of the gore of battle turns them off, or they find it too scary or not like their idea of how God deals with His creation. But if they close the book at this point, they'll miss the comforting message of God's defeat of evil and the final establishment of God's eternal kingdom.

In Revelation 19:11, Jesus leads the armies of heaven riding on a white horse, and he's called Faithful and True, and it says that he judges and makes war with justice. Why justice? It's because throughout the book of Revelation we've found the recurring theme that God is very patient, and always ready to take people back. He has no desire that people should suffer, and all through the times of tribulation has been seeking people out in love and compassion. But some people will not change. They will not give up following the beast known as Antichrist. They prefer his message filled with lies, his value of self-centeredness, his way that leads to death, over the message of truth, the value of other-centeredness, and the way leading to life that comes from God. And so, they end up following Antichrist to their doom. With all this buildup about how powerful the Antichrist is on earth, his end in verse 20 seems like an after-thought. The beast and the false prophet that we saw introduced in Chapter 13 are thrown into a lake of fire that burns forever. That's where we get our picture of Hell as a fiery place inhabited by demons. Of course, we knew all along that they would be defeated, so it's not a surprise.

Or is it? How many times have you thought that the world was going to Hell in a hand-basket? How often have you despaired of the increase in crime, drug use, disease, and abortion? Have there been times when you've wondered if it's worth it to be a Christian, to be honest and decent, to try and love unlovable people on the job? We do have the right to choose after all. We have our free will to conduct our lives as we wish. So, why choose one over the other, when being a Christian, and having a focus on Christ and His way can sometimes seem so confining? We all know people who seem to have chosen to follow the pathway of lies, deceit, confusion, and a series of destructive relationships. Why do people choose to do that? Jesus told a parable about the kingdom of heaven and the choices we make that I think applies to this chapter in Revelation. Read Matthew 22:1-14 to hear Jesus' parable of the Kingdom of God and the choices we make to join it or not.

¹ "Jesus answered and spoke to them again in parables, saying, ² "The Kingdom of Heaven is like a certain king, who made a marriage feast for his son, ³ and sent out his servants to call those who were invited to the marriage feast, but they would not come. ⁴ Again he sent out other servants, saying, 'Tell those who are invited, "Behold, I have prepared my dinner. My cattle and my fatlings are killed, and all things are ready. Come to the marriage feast!"' ⁵ But they made light of it, and went their ways, one to his own farm, another to his merchandise, ⁶ and the rest grabbed his servants, and treated them shamefully, and killed them. ⁷ When the king heard that, he was angry, and sent his armies, destroyed those murderers, and burned their city.

⁸ "Then he said to his servants, 'The wedding is ready, but those who were invited weren't worthy. ⁹ Go therefore to the intersections of the highways, and as many as you may find, invite to the marriage feast.' ¹⁰ Those servants went out into the highways, and gathered together as many as they found, both bad and good. The wedding was filled with guests. ¹¹ But when the king came in to see the guests, he saw there a man who didn't have on wedding clothing, ¹² and he said to him, 'Friend, how did you come in here not wearing wedding clothing?' He was speechless. ¹³ Then the king said to the servants, 'Bind him hand and foot, take him away, and throw him into the outer darkness. That is where the weeping and grinding of teeth will be.' ¹⁴ For many are called, but few chosen." (Matthew 22:1-14)

In this parable, which Jesus says is about the kingdom of heaven, and likens it to a king who prepares a wedding feast for his son. He invites many people, but they refuse to come. He sends servants with a message from him inviting them to the wedding banquet. But they spurn his invitation, some say they are too busy in their fields, or in their businesses, as we see in Matthew 22:5. Some abuse and kill the servants. The king becomes enraged and sends out his army to destroy those who murdered his servants, and then sends more servants out into the streets to invite everyone into the feast. For the original invitees, the issue really was that they chose not to come. For the next group, who were invited in off the streets, not everyone who came was properly attired, as we see in Matthew 22:11. They didn't meet the requirements for entry into the wedding feast. In other words, they may have wanted to enter the kingdom of heaven, but they came without putting on the garments of righteousness and faith, which are symbolized by the fine linen of the bride in Revelation, proper for guests at the heavenly banquet.

When it comes to the kingdom of God, we have only two choices: we can reject it outright and receive the consequences of that choice, or we can come into it through faith in Jesus Christ and join in the celebration of the victory over evil. We have a choice of a feast in heaven where we are the guests, or the feast on earth where we are the victims. Some people might hear this chapter in Revelation and decide to believe in Christ because they want join in the celebration in heaven. Others might hear this chapter and decide to believe in Christ because they are afraid of Hell. In both cases, the important decision is choosing to make their Christ Savior and Lord.

STUDY QUESTIONS

Q: No matter how you structure Revelation, what do you think is the main theme John wants us to get from it?

Q: What is God angry about?

Q: How do you reconcile the angry God of 15:7 with the righteous God of verse 15:4?

Q: What motivated you to become a believer?

20

MILLENNIUM AND JUDGEMENT

What I've been trying to do in this guide for understanding is give you an overview of the book of Revelation, not a detailed word for word study. I've also resisted putting Revelation into a timeline for the future because I've wanted to let John speak to us directly, without letting what we might have heard previously cause us to miss his real message. But people throughout the ages have been curious about what the future might hold, and have tried to organize the Bible into a consistent pattern. Over the centuries, interpreters have come up with a number of different ways to understand what's going on in chapter 20, with its introduction of a 1000 year period known as the Millennium followed by the destruction of Satan and the Last Judgment, and how they fit with the rest of the book in an overall plan.

REVELATION 20:1-15

¹ "I saw an angel coming down out of heaven, having the key of the abyss and a great chain in his hand. ² He seized the dragon, the old serpent, which is the devil and Satan, who deceives the whole inhabited earth, and bound him for a thousand years, ³ and cast him into the abyss, and shut it, and sealed it over him, that he should deceive the nations no more, until the thousand years were finished. After this, he must be freed for a short time. *4 I saw thrones, and they sat on them, and judgment was given to them. I saw the souls of those who had been beheaded for the testimony of Jesus, and for the word of God, and such as didn't worship the beast nor his image, and didn't receive the mark on their forehead and on their hand. They lived and reigned with Christ for a thousand years. 5 The rest of the dead didn't live until the thousand years were finished. This is the first resurrection. 6 Blessed and holy is he who has part in the first resurrection. Over these, the second death has no power, but they will be priests of God and of Christ, and will reign with him one thousand years.*

7 And after the thousand years, Satan will be released from his prison, 8 and he will come out to deceive the nations which are in the four corners of the earth, Gog and Magog, to gather them together to the war; the number of whom is as the sand of the sea. 9 They went up over the width of the earth, and surrounded the camp of the saints, and the beloved city. Fire came down out of heaven from God and devoured them. 10 The devil who deceived them was thrown into the lake of fire and sulfur, where the beast and the false prophet are also. They will be tormented day and night forever and ever.

11 I saw a great white throne, and him who sat on it, from whose face the earth and the heaven fled away. There was found no place for them. 12 I saw the dead, the great and the small, standing before the throne, and they opened books. Another book was opened, which is the book of life. The dead were judged out of the things which were written in the books, according to their works. 13 The sea gave up the dead who were in it. Death and Hades gave up the dead who were in them. They were judged, each one according to his works. 14 Death and Hades were thrown into the lake of fire. This is the second death, the lake of fire. ¹⁵ *If anyone was not found written in the book of life, he was cast into the lake of fire.*"

You may have heard words such as "premillennial" or "post-millennial," "dispensational," or "a-millennial," to label various plans for the future. Chapter 20 is key to figuring out those terms when it introduces a thousand-year period of peace with Jesus and some of the Christian martyrs ruling the world. The question being debated concerning those plans is whether the Millennium is yet to come, or has begun already, or has been completed. If it already has come, then the Tribulation described in previous chapters has also occurred. If the Millennium is yet to come, then the Tribulation is yet to come, or we're already in it.

Another debated question is exactly when do Christians join Jesus in His Kingdom: before, during or after the Tribulation. This, of course, assumes that there is a specific time-period of struggle and oppression known as the Tribulation that greatly exceeds any previous time of trouble. Theologians define the time when Christ comes again and takes Christians to heaven out of their everyday lives, as the Rapture. Adding the Rapture to the plan for the future leads to even more options called pre-Tribulation rapture, post-Tribulation rapture, or mid-Tribulation rapture, depending on when this Rapture event occurs.

In a surprise to many, the word "rapture" doesn't occur in our English Bibles. It is derived from the Latin word, *rapiemur*, which is in the Vulgate version of the Bible at I Thessalonians 4:17 to translate "we will be caught up." In another surprise, this Rapture event is not mentioned as such in the book of Revelation. As we mentioned when we looked at chapter 15, it appears that all believers are in Heaven praising God in chapter 15, having been reaped from Earth in chapter 14, so this Rapture could have occurred prior to when the bowls of wrath are poured out on the unbelieving world in chapter 16. In the "Left Behind" series of books, this Rapture happens right at the beginning of the first volume, where the hero finds his wife and child have disappeared. They were believers, but he was not, so he was "left behind," along with everyone else on earth who had not come to faith in Christ. There are a few passages in the New Testament where such an event is prophesied.

Look at Mark 13:26-27 to see what Jesus said about the rapture of believers.

26 "Then they will see the Son of Man coming in clouds with great power and glory. 27 Then he will send out his angels, and will gather together his chosen ones from the four winds, from the ends of the earth to the ends of the sky." (Mark 13:26-27)

"Coming in the clouds" refers back to Daniel 7:13, where Daniel saw a vision of the Lord as the Son of Man coming in the clouds of heaven to establish his kingdom.

13 "I saw in the night visions, and behold, there came with the clouds of the sky one like a son of man, and he came even to the ancient of days, and they brought him near before him." (Daniel 7:13)

This leads us back to Revelation 14:14-16 where the Son of Man, sitting on a cloud, wields a sickle to reap the Earth, and it seems like He was reaping believers because in the next section of chapter 14, an angel reaps those destined for the wrath of God.

The Apostle Paul expanded on this event in his letters to the Thessalonians and the Corinthians to answer a concern some of them had that those who die before Christ comes might miss out on spending eternity with God. Look at I Thessalonians 4:13-17 to see what Paul said about the rapture of believers who had died.

13 "But we don't want you to be ignorant, brothers, concerning those who have fallen asleep, so that you don't grieve like the rest, who have no hope. 14 For if we believe that Jesus died and rose again, even so God will bring with him those who have fallen asleep in Jesus. 15 For this we tell you by the word of the Lord, that we who are alive, who are left until the coming of the Lord, will in no way precede those who have fallen asleep. 16 For the Lord himself will descend from heaven with a shout, with the voice of the archangel, and with God's trumpet. The dead in Christ will rise first, 17 then we who are alive, who are left, will be caught up together with them in the clouds, to meet the Lord in the air. So we will be with the Lord forever." (I Thessalonians 4:13-17)

Now look at I Corinthians 15:51-52 where Paul summarized this raising of the dead believers.

51 "Behold, I tell you a mystery. We will not all sleep, but we will all be changed, 52 in a moment, in the twinkling of an eye, at the last trumpet. For the trumpet will sound, and the dead will be raised incorruptible, and we will be changed." (I Corinthians 15:51-52)

From passages like this, theologians deduced that Christians alive at Christ's return would not die, but be taken to be with Him in heaven. But that left the question of whether that event, which they called the "Rapture," happened before the Tribulation, after it, or in the middle of it. That also involves the question whether the Tribulation already happened or is yet to happen. The various divisions and subdivisions of a theological understanding of the future can lead to lively debate, but for the purposes of our study, I think we can boil them down into two basic positions on when the Millennium, or thousand-year period, occurs in history.

The first group says that the Millennium will happen some time in the future. The second group says we're already in it. The first group takes Jesus' promises of a Kingdom of God, and says although some aspects of the Kingdom of God are already here, there's a lot more to it that we certainly aren't experiencing. There's too much evil in this world for it to be the Kingdom of God already come with power and glory like we read about in the Bible.

The second group takes the same promises of Jesus, and says that since Jesus said that Kingdom of God is among us and in our hearts, it's already come. The Millennium isn't merely a fixed 1000 year period, but stands for an indefinite period of time when the Kingdom of God is active on earth in the lives of men and women of faith. Christ started it by defeating Satan by dying for our sins on the cross and rising from the dead, and Jesus is ruling right now. And if it doesn't seem to us that God is in charge of this world, it's because we Christians aren't doing our job to the fullest to help Jesus remake this world into the Kingdom of God.

Now, I want to emphasize that both of these positions, that the Millennium is in the future, and that the

Millennium has already begun, have been held by fervent evangelical Christians in the past and up to today. Each side has valid reasons to support its position, and most honest interpreters, no matter which side they are on, will admit that there are holes and inconsistencies in both positions. For example, the first position has the problem explaining why Satan is bound for a thousand years in Revelation 20:3 and then let loose again for another battle with God in Revelation 20:8 before he is finally thrown into the lake of fire in verse 10. Why isn't Satan disposed of the first time he's captured? The second position solves that by saying that Satan is bound by God right now so the gospel can be spread to the whole world, and if he wasn't bound, we couldn't do it at all. But this position also has a problem in that it doesn't explain exactly who and where these Christian martyrs are we see in Revelation 20:4 who have been resurrected to rule during the Millennium, which the interpreters of the first position have no problem explaining because it's still off in the future.

The bottom line is there are still a lot of things we don't know and aren't told. There's a whole lot of detail about the future that God hasn't chosen to reveal to us, even though he gave us a partial glimpse of it through John's visions that he recorded here. A wise Christian approaches the subject of Eschatology, or Last Things, with humility, not arrogance, and admits that there are a lot of loose ends to any approach. Which I actually think is reasonable, because it gives God the freedom to conduct the future as He sees fit, rather than the way I would like it to play out. We tend to construct a system so that we come out on top. Jesus said that He Himself did not know the time when He would return in power and glory. Look again at Matthew 24:36 where Jesus says no one knows except God Himself.

24 *"But about that day or hour no one knows, not even the angels in heaven, nor the Son, but only the Father." (Matthew 24:36)*

So what does it matter, which approach you take to the future, or if you choose to ignore it all together? For one thing, the position that churches have taken has affected how they understand their mission in the world. If a church takes the first position that the Millennium is only future, they might de-emphasize doing good works today because the present world is under the influence of Satan, and until he's out of the way, it's fruitless activity. So, a Christian life based on Jesus' teachings in the Sermon on the Mount is more or less impossible to accomplish in this present age, and is only feasible in the Millennium when Satan is bound and Christ is in control of the world. The goal of the church for them is not so much to make the world a better place to live, but primarily to bring as many people to faith in Christ as possible before he returns as a Militant Messiah and Judge.

If a church takes the second position, that the Millennium already started at Christ's death and Resurrection when Satan's power was broken, they might emphasize that the role of the church is to carry out the mission of Christ in making this present world the Kingdom of God on Earth. Evangelism is good, but so is doing good works right now. The job of the church is to make the world a place worthy enough and pure enough for Jesus' return as King of King and Lord of Lords. And even with the help of the Holy Spirit, we've still got a long way to go.

As is so often the case in scripture, it may not be a situation of either-or; that you have to adopt one position at the expense of the other. It may be better to take a position of both-and, where the truth lies in both positions at the same time. Yes, Satan was defeated at the cross, and so his power was diminished, and, Yes, Satan still has power that will only be finally overcome by Christ's return. And, Yes, the Kingdom of God comes to earth in the hearts of men and women who respond to Jesus' call, and Yes, it won't come in all its fullness until some point in the future.

Going past the verses discussing the Millennium and Satan's final destruction in the Lake of Fire in verse 10, in Revelation 20:11, we see the Day of Judgment in verses 12 and 13, where all the dead stand before God and are judged. The prophet Daniel also had a vision of the Day of Judgment, with God seated on His throne, opening books.

9 *"I watched until thrones were placed,*
   and one who was ancient of days sat.
His clothing was white as snow,
   and the hair of his head like pure wool.
His throne was fiery flames,
   and its wheels burning fire.
10 *A fiery stream issued and came out from before him.*
   Thousands of thousands ministered to him.
Ten thousand times ten thousand stood before him.
   The judgment was set. The books were
opened." (Daniel 7:9-10)

The Ancient of Days is God himself seated on His heavenly throne surrounded by fire, served by thousands of heavenly beings, and sitting in judgment on millions of human beings. And He opens books that will help Him make those judgments.

From Revelation 20:12-13, we can see there are actually two kinds of judgment to be made. First, there's a judgment based on what we've done. The books that contain the records of our lives are opened to see whether what we did was good or bad, righteous or unrighteous, holy or unholy. But, if you follow the way the text reads, it seems to suggest that this isn't how God decides to send us to Heaven or Hell. That decision seems to be made on the contents of another book, the book of life. If our names are not found there, verse 15 says, then we are thrown into the lake of fire to join the devil, the Antichrist, and death and Hades. Some churches have focused on this book of life and made it the sole deciding factor as to whether you will spend eternity in Heaven with God or in Hell with Satan. Some have said your name was written there by God before the world began and nothing you do can change that; others have said your name is written there only when you come to faith in Jesus Christ as Lord and Savior; others have you sign a book when you join their church to symbolize your name being written in the heavenly book as well. The only thing the text says is if your name is not written in the book of life, you go to Hell. It does not say what happens when the books containing the actions of our lives are opened and we stand before God for judgment.

Jesus talked to His disciples about what happens on Judgment Day in Matthew 25:31-46.

31 "But when the Son of Man comes in his glory, and all the holy angels with him, then he will sit on the throne of his glory. 32 Before him all the nations will be gathered, and he will separate them one from another, as a shepherd separates the sheep from the goats. 33 He will set the sheep on his right hand, but the goats on the left. 34 Then the King will tell those on his right hand, 'Come, blessed of my Father, inherit the Kingdom prepared for you from the foundation of the world; 35 for I was hungry, and you gave me food to eat. I was thirsty, and you gave me drink. I was a stranger, and you took me in. 36 I was naked, and you clothed me. I was sick, and you visited me. I was in prison, and you came to me.'

37 "Then the righteous will answer him, saying, 'Lord, when did we see you hungry, and feed you; or thirsty, and give you a drink? 38 When did we see you as a stranger, and take you in; or naked, and clothe you? 39 When did we see you sick, or in prison, and come to you?' 40 "The King will answer them, 'Most certainly I tell you, because you did it to one of the least of these my brothers,‡ you did it to me.' 41 Then he will say also to those on the left hand, 'Depart from me, you cursed, into the eternal fire which is prepared for the devil and his angels; 42 for I was hungry, and you didn't give me food to eat; I was thirsty, and you gave me no drink; 43 I was a stranger, and you didn't take me in; naked, and you didn't clothe me; sick, and in prison, and you didn't visit me.' 44 "Then they will also answer, saying, 'Lord, when did we see you hungry, or thirsty, or a stranger, or naked, or sick, or in prison, and didn't help you?' 45 "Then he will answer them, saying, 'Most certainly I tell you, because you didn't do it to one of the least of these, you didn't do it to me.' 46 These will go away into eternal punishment, but the righteous into eternal life." (Matthew 25:31-46)

Jesus made a special point that a person's behavior will be considered on Judgment Day: If you feed the hungry and thirsty, if you give clothes to those who need them, if you visit the sick and take care of them, if you visit those in prison, then you are called blessed by God, and will inherit the eternal Kingdom of God. If you do not do those things, then you will receive eternal punishment. Based on this story from Jesus, I think we can conclude that our faith in Jesus Christ AND our good works are both important to God. We can have all the good works in the world, but if we don't have faith, we won't pass the exam on Judgment Day. And if we have tons of faith, but no good works flow out of that faith, we may not pass either.

21

A NEW HEAVEN AND A NEW EARTH

John has done an amazing thing in writing Revelation the way he did. He wrote it much as a writer today might write a mystery or adventure story, starting out with describing the general scene of the action, giving us a few clues to whet our appetite, then gradually building the action and suspense until we reach the final climatic scene, where the bad guys get their just deserts, the destruction they've caused gets fixed, and the good guys live happily ever after. In Chapter 20, we saw the last battle won and the bad guys sent to the abyss where they are tormented for eternity. In Chapter 21, the destruction they've caused gets fixed with a new heaven and a new earth, and the good guys, the believers in Christ, live in blessed fellowship with God for eternity. Revelation chapter 21 describes how God recreates a perfect world where He and believers will be in fellowship forever.

REVELATION 21:1-27

¹ "I saw a new heaven and a new earth: for the first heaven and the first earth have passed away, and the sea is no more. ² I saw the holy city, New Jerusalem, coming down out of heaven from God, prepared like a bride adorned for her husband. ³ I heard a loud voice out of heaven saying, "Behold, God's dwelling is with people, and he will dwell with them, and they will be his people, and God himself will be with them as their God. ⁴ He will wipe away every tear from their eyes. Death will be no more; neither will there be mourning, nor crying, nor pain, any more. The first things have passed away."

⁵ He who sits on the throne said, "Behold, I am making all things new." He said, "Write, for these words of God are faithful and true." ⁶ He said to me, "I have become the Alpha and the Omega, the Beginning and the End. I will give freely to him who is thirsty from the spring of the water of life. ⁷ He who overcomes, I will give him these things. I will be his God, and he will be my son. ⁸ But for the cowardly, unbelieving, sinners, abominable, murderers, sexually immoral, sorcerers, idolaters, and all liars, their part is in the lake that burns with fire and sulfur, which is the second death."

⁹ One of the seven angels who had the seven bowls, who were loaded with the seven last plagues came, and he spoke with me, saying, "Come here. I will show you the wife, the Lamb's bride." ¹⁰ He carried me away in the Spirit to a great and high mountain, and showed me the holy city, Jerusalem, coming down out of heaven from God, ¹¹ having the glory of God. Her light was like a most precious stone, as if it were a jasper stone, clear as crystal; ¹² having a great and high wall; having twelve gates, and at the gates twelve angels; and names written on them, which are the names of the twelve tribes of the children of Israel. ¹³ On the east were three gates; and on the north three gates; and on the south three gates; and on the west three gates. ¹⁴ The wall of the city had twelve foundations, and on them twelve names of the twelve Apostles of the Lamb. ¹⁵ He who spoke with me had for a measure a golden reed to measure the city, its gates, and its walls. ¹⁶ The city is

square, and its length is as great as its width. He measured the city with the reed, twelve thousand twelve stadia. Its length, width, and height are equal. *17 Its wall is one hundred forty-four cubits, by the measure of a man, that is, of an angel. 18 The construction of its wall was jasper. The city was pure gold, like pure glass. 19 The foundations of the city's wall were adorned with all kinds of precious stones. The first foundation was jasper; the second, sapphire; the third, chalcedony; the fourth, emerald; 20 the fifth, sardonyx; the sixth, sardius; the seventh, chrysolite; the eighth, beryl; the ninth, topaz; the tenth, chrysoprasus; the eleventh, jacinth; and the twelfth, amethyst. 21 The twelve gates were twelve pearls. Each one of the gates was made of one pearl. The street of the city was pure gold, like transparent glass. 22 I saw no temple in it, for the Lord God, the Almighty, and the Lamb, are its temple. 23 The city has no need for the sun, neither of the moon, to shine, for the very glory of God illuminated it, and its lamp is the Lamb. 24 The nations will walk in its light. The kings of the earth bring the glory and honor of the nations into it. 25 Its gates will in no way be shut by day (for there will be no night there), 26 and they shall bring the glory and the honor of the nations into it so that they may enter. 27 There will in no way enter into it anything profane, or one who causes an abomination or a lie, but only those who are written in the Lamb's book of life."*

A significant discovery that may have struck you about the book of Revelation as we went through each chapter, is that John has wrapped up in the course of his writing most of the Old Testament prophecies of the coming reign of the Messiah, the Day of the Lord, and the future paradise on Earth where God lives with His people. For John, this series of visions decisively fulfills all those prophecies. This is the high point of all history, the culmination of everything that God has been doing on Earth with His people. This is where the Kingdom of God you read about in both the Old Testament and in the Gospels becomes reality. A New Jerusalem symbolizing the totality of God's glory replaces the Old Jerusalem that symbolizes the depravity of mankind. A Holy City replaces an unholy realm to become a place where God can dwell among His people.

The Old Testament contains a number of prophecies of what the future heavenly paradise will be like. The prophet Isaiah said:

> [17] *"For, behold, I create new heavens and a new earth;*
> *and the former things will not be remembered,*
> *nor come into mind.*
> [18] *But be glad and rejoice forever in that which I create;*
> *for, behold, I create Jerusalem to be a delight,*
> *and her people a joy.*
> [19] *I will rejoice in Jerusalem, and delight in my people;*
> *and the voice of weeping and the voice of crying*
> *will be heard in her no more."*

> [20] *"No more will there be an infant who only lives a few*
> *days, nor an old man who has not filled his days;*
> *for the child will die one hundred years old,*
> *and the sinner being one hundred years old will be*
> *accursed." (Isaiah 65:17-20)*

In Isaiah 65:17, we see a new heaven and a new earth; a New Jerusalem that is a delight; no more weeping and crying, and everyone will live for a very long time, which is exactly what Revelation 21:4 says.

Now look at Leviticus 26:11-12, Jeremiah 31:33, and Ezekiel 37:26-27, to see how those prophecies are fulfilled by John's vision.

11 "I will set my tent among you, and my soul won't abhor you. 12 I will walk among you, and will be your God, and you will be my people." (Leviticus 26:11-12)

33 "But this is the covenant that I will make with the house of Israel after those days," says Yahweh: "I will put my law in their inward parts, and I will write it in their heart. I will be their God, and they shall be my people." (Jeremiah 31:33)

26 "Moreover I will make a covenant of peace with them. It will be an everlasting covenant with them. I will place them, multiply them, and will set my sanctuary among them forever more. 27 My tent also will be with them. I will be their God, and they will be my people." (Ezekiel 37:26-27)

The New Jerusalem is really John's picture of what heaven is like, since it's the place where all the believers live for eternity. And God lives among them. It's not much different than the picture we get in Genesis of Adam and Eve walking in the Garden of Eden with God. The Garden of Eden was paradise just as much as Heaven is paradise. Heaven is returning to the way God created the world originally, where He is God and we are His people, and the world exists in peace and harmony. The last book of the Bible, Revelation, ends up where the first book of the Bible, Genesis, began.

A question that may come to mind is, "How can the New Jerusalem be the bride of Christ?" We saw the

wedding supper of Christ in chapter 19, and there I said
that the bride symbolized the church because her wedding
dress was the righteous deeds of the saints. We didn't dwell
on how the picture of a wedding between Christ and all of
us made sense. It sounds like some sort of group marriage
between Christ and millions of men and women, and it just
doesn't compute. And this image in Revelation 21 of Christ
marrying a city doesn't quite compute, either. We might as
well be talking about marrying a desk or a chair or a house,
none of which make sense. But we have to remember that
John is more of an artist than an engineer. He was giving
us pictures, not construction blueprints. Chapter 21 shows
the New Jerusalem as the place where believers live in
God's presence. The gold and jewels are there only to say
that this is a very precious and glorious place to be. The
wedding here and in chapter 19 symbolizes the deep love
Christ has for us and the possibility for us to have closeness
and intimate communion with Him.

Another question that came to my mind was, "The
Bible says that God is everywhere already, and He is
already our God and we are His people. So what's going to
be different in this heavenly existence?" One of the
differences is who's going to be in this city, and who isn't.
Revelation 21:7 tells us that overcomers will inherit the
city, referring back to chapters 2 and 3 where Jesus,
through John, exhorted members of the churches of Asia to
overcome the pressures to follow Satan and stay true to
God. Revelation 21:27 tells us that no impurity will enter
this city, nor anyone who does shameful or deceitful things,
but only those whose names are written in the book of life.

On the other hand, verse 8 gives a list of those who
definitely won't be there. I am always amazed by the awful
things people can do to each other. I once read a story in

the newspaper about a woman in Baltimore a number of years ago who admitted setting fire to her house to kill her 2 and 4 year old daughters. And then there was a woman in Tallahassee who told her husband of 6 months that she wanted a divorce. While she was napping, her husband came in, poured gasoline over her, and set her on fire. I cannot comprehend how people can put such a low value on human life that they can so callously snuff out someone else's. I don't know if such incidents are on the increase, or if there really hasn't been any change over the centuries except media willing to report stories like these. I do believe that people like this would not be able to tolerate being in the presence of God. They couldn't stand the power of His righteousness or the awesomeness of His holiness. Maybe that's why the city described in Revelation 21 is lit by His Glory, rather than the sun or moon or electricity. God's Glory is a light that shines in the darkness, as Isaiah foretold, that eliminates the darkness entirely, including the darkness that lies deep in our souls. The darkness that's been there since Cain slew Abel, that allows us to do such awful things to our fellow human beings, is gone.

Note also, that there is no temple in the New Jerusalem. In the Old Jerusalem, the temple was the centerpiece. I have a picture of the present temple mount hanging over my desk, which King Herod the Great built to have a level place for the new temple that he also built. The temple mount is immense and the temple itself must have been huge when it existed. Josephus, the Jewish historian of the first century, tells us that Herod's temple "was covered all over with plates of gold of great weight, and at the first rising of the sun, reflected back a very fiery splendor, and made those who forced themselves to look upon it to turn away their eyes, just as they would at the sun's own rays. But this temple appeared to strangers, when they were at a distance, like a mountain covered with snow, for as to those parts that were not golden, they were exceedingly white." The temple was one of the seven wonders of the ancient world. It was the center of life in Palestine. There are those who think that it needs to be built again to satisfy prophecy, but from John's point of view, the temple was only a temporary monument, a symbol rather than the reality of God's presence. When God lives among his people as we see here in Revelation 21, there's no need for any man-made building, no matter how beautiful, to serve as a worship center, because you can worship God right where you are.

OUR FUTURE HOPE

As we complete our study of John's letter, which he wrote around 95 AD to bring comfort to members of the churches in Asia, we need to remember that he tried to help them understand what was happening to them. After all, they expected that God would do something to stop the Roman persecution that was arresting Christians for their faith and executing them or sending them off to prison. Didn't Jesus teach that the Kingdom of God had come? So where is it? Read Revelation chapter 22 to hear John's answer to the questions of when and where is the Kingdom of God?

REVELATION 22:1-21

¹ *"He showed me a river of water of life, clear as crystal, proceeding out of the throne of God and of the Lamb,* ² *in the middle of its street. On this side of the river and on that was the tree of life, bearing twelve kinds of fruits, yielding its fruit every month. The leaves of the tree were for the healing of the nations.* ³ *There will be no curse any more. The throne of God and of the Lamb will be in it, and his servants will serve him.* ⁴ *They will see his face, and his name will be on their foreheads.* ⁵ *There will be no night, and they need no lamp light; for the Lord God will illuminate them. They will reign forever and ever.*

⁶ He said to me, "These words are faithful and true. The Lord God of the spirits of the prophets sent his angel to show to his bondservants the things which must happen soon." ⁷ "Behold, I come quickly. Blessed is he who keeps the words of the prophecy of this book."

⁸ Now I, John, am the one who heard and saw these things. When I heard and saw, I fell down to worship before the feet of the angel who had shown me these things. ⁹ He said to me, "See you don't do it! I am a fellow bondservant with you and with your brothers, the prophets, and with those who keep the words of this book. Worship God." ¹⁰ He said to me, "Don't seal up the words of the prophecy of this book, for the time is at hand. ¹¹ He who acts unjustly, let him act unjustly still. He who is filthy, let him be filthy still. He who is righteous, let him do righteousness still. He who is holy, let him be holy still."

¹² "Behold, I come quickly. My reward is with me, to repay to each man according to his work. ¹³ I am the Alpha and the Omega, the First and the Last, the Beginning and the End. ¹⁴ Blessed are those who do his commandments,† that they may have the right to the tree of life, and may enter in by the gates into the city. ¹⁵ Outside are the dogs, the sorcerers, the sexually immoral, the murderers, the idolaters, and everyone who loves and practices falsehood. ¹⁶ I, Jesus, have sent my angel to testify these things to you for the assemblies. I am the root and the offspring of David; the Bright and Morning Star."

¹⁷ The Spirit and the bride say, "Come!" He who hears, let him say, "Come!" He who is thirsty, let him come. He who desires, let him take the water of life freely. ¹⁸ I

testify to everyone who hears the words of the prophecy of this book, if anyone adds to them, may God add to him the plagues which are written in this book. ¹⁹ If anyone takes away from the words of the book of this prophecy, may God take away his part from the tree of life, and out of the holy city, which are written in this book. ²⁰ He who testifies these things says, "Yes, I come quickly." Amen! Yes, come, Lord Jesus.

²¹ The grace of the Lord Jesus Christ be with all the saints. Amen."

John's answer, as we saw in Chapter 1, and see here again in verses 7 and 20, is that Jesus is coming back soon. As we saw in reading through Revelation, "soon" is a relative term, because the course of events in Revelation goes through three series of plagues and disasters that we called the Tribulation, before the start of a thousand year period of peace we called the Millennium. Between the two, Jesus returns and defeats the evil political empire bringing an end to the persecution. And after the Millennium, the Devil is sent to join his supporters in Hell, and God recreates a new heaven and a new earth.

I have to admit that Revelation is a difficult book to study and understand. There are some chapters in Revelation that I don't particularly like to read and study — chapters that talk about many-headed monsters and a dragon, and believers being killed for their faith. As I studied Revelation, I sometimes wondered if John was having nightmares rather than visions. But having come out the other side, I can look back on all that unpleasant stuff and realize that it was a necessary part of the story. You can't have the peace and harmony of heaven unless the Devil who seeks to prevent peace and harmony is

destroyed. When you step back and take a look at the
whole book, you see that it's really an epic story with
powerful themes: the struggle between good and evil; the
faithfulness of believers who choose life with God over
death with Satan; and the power of God and His Messiah
over the whole creation.

You'd think that choosing to be an overcomer, to
choose life with God over death with Satan would be an
easy choice. But we've seen in Revelation that while God
offers life over and over to people, that time and time again
many turn Him down. But for those who do choose life,
their lives became eternal lives that supersede death.
Eternal life is symbolized in verse 2 and 14, where we read
about the tree of life, which takes us back once again to the
Garden of Eden. If you recall from the Creation story in
Genesis 2 and 3, God planted a garden, and in it He put a
man and a woman, whose sole purpose in life was to have
fellowship with Him, to walk and talk in the garden.
Apparently, companionship is very important to God,
because in Genesis 2:16, He says to himself, "It is not good
for man to be alone," so He created Eve to be Adam's
companion. You may also recall that there were two trees
in that garden that were very special. One was the tree of
the knowledge of good and evil, which they were told not to
eat of its fruit. But the other tree was the tree of life, and
apparently they could eat of the fruit of that tree. One day
Satan came along and decided to mess up this peace and
harmony by tempting Eve to eat the forbidden fruit and
become like God herself. She ate the apple and so did
Adam, but they didn't become like God at all. In fact, they
became more like Satan and began to lie and blame each
other. When God found out, He was upset that the humans
He'd made had spoiled paradise, so He decided to kick
them out of the garden, so that they couldn't "take from the

tree of life and live forever," as it says in Genesis 3:22. Figuratively, our limited life span comes from our not being able to eat from the tree of life. And yet, here in Revelation 22, in the new heaven and new earth, there will be trees of life for us to eat from, and rivers of life for us to drink from, all over the place. In other words, we're back in the Garden of Eden, we're restored to eternal life and eternal fellowship with God.

In Revelation 22, there are many promises to believers who stay the course and don't hide from professing Christ. We are promised eternal life if we are cleansed by our faith in Jesus Christ. That's what it means in verse 14 where it says that those who wash their robes will have access to the tree of life. And in verse 3 we are promised that the world will no longer be under the curse of our sin, which darkens the world. Instead, in verse 5, we read that there will be no more night because God himself with be our light. And we will reign with Him for ever and ever. This idea of sitting on thrones, and having some sort of rulership over the earth is a common theme in Revelation and the Old Testament. It's such a contrast to what the early Christians were experiencing, where the rulers were oppressive Romans, and the Christians were fed to lions. The desire for freedom to make your own way in the world without anyone telling you what to do and not do, seems to lie deep in the human experience: Hebrew slaves in Egypt longed to be free; Black slaves in the 19th century United States longed to be free; Russians longed to determine their own destiny. But, here in our future heavenly home, our freedom is granted by God. To some people today, to have your freedom determined by God might seem restrictive, but frankly, I'm looking forward to it, because it will be the rule of perfect divine grace rather than the rule of imperfect human law.

Verses 10 and 11 need an explanation. Verse 10 says that John is not to seal up the contents of this book for the time is near. That is opposite to the instruction given to Daniel in Daniel 8:26, where he was told to seal up his book containing his visions, because the time was far off. John's revelations are to be given to the believing world so that it can have an effect on their behavior. If that's the case, verse 11, makes no sense. It seems to imply that we should let evil people stay evil, and righteous people stay righteous. That would mean there's no need for evangelism; let the bad people proceed on their merry way to hell, while we Christians ignore their plight. I don't think that's what the angel meant. Commentators for the most part don't know exactly how to interpret this verse, but I think its significance lies in coming immediately between a verse that says the time is near, and a verse where Jesus says, "I am coming quickly."

The key word is the word "time." In Greek, there are two words for time, *kronos*, and *kairos*. *Kronos* has to do with clock time, minutes and seconds. If John had said the *kronos* is near, we would know he was talking about a specific date and hour for Jesus' return. But he didn't use the word *kronos*. He used the word *kairos*, which isn't clock time at all. *Kairos* means that all the conditions for Jesus' coming are in place, the situation is right for his return. We often say, "The times are right for something to happen," which has the same meaning as John uses here. If the times are right for the Lord's return, letting the evil people stay evil might be John's way of saying that there's nothing evil people can do to stop or postpone Jesus' coming. It's out of their power because it's in God's power and God's time. John's message is that Jesus is coming, don't be discouraged by the evil you see, because no matter how bad the oppressors are, they can't stop the power of the Lord; they can't delay His coming. When we talk about the Lord's return, we've left our clock time, and moved into God's time. On the other hand, if it's God's timing for the Lord's return, there's nothing good people can do that will hasten it. I can imagine, if I were an early Christian on my way to the arena to fight some lions, that I might want the Lord to return immediately to save me from being torn apart. John's message is that Jesus is coming, don't be discouraged, but He might not be coming in clock time to save you and me from the jaws of the lions.

As John brings his letter to a close, Jesus reminds us three times in verses 7, 12, and 20 that He is coming soon. In verse 16, we see John including a closing statement by Jesus himself about the validity of John's writing. This letter isn't valid just because John reported what he saw in visions as if he were writing for a newspaper. No, this letter is valid because it comes to you through John from Jesus himself. Jesus reminds us that He is the root and offspring of David, the Messiah promised in the Old Testament prophecies, and the bright Morning Star, the sign of a new age. To that John can only respond by saying "Come." In verse 17, the Spirit says "Come," and the bride, which is the church composed of believers says "Come." You're long overdue, Jesus, this world needs You now. And to those readers or hearers who are not believers, John says that "whoever is thirsty, let him come and partake of the free gift of the water of life that comes from God." John then offers a warning to anyone who might be so bold as to modify what he has written down, either by adding something to it, or subtracting something from it. This letter of his is essentially the final word of prophecy to God's people because it sums up all the prophecies of Old and New testaments about the coming of God's kingdom in the hearts of men and women, and in the history of the world. There's nothing more needed to be said, only to be believed.

Verse 20 adds one last reminder from Jesus, "Yes, I am coming soon." To which John can only reply, "Amen, so be it. Come, Lord Jesus." And then verse 21 provides a final blessing from John on God's people everywhere who read this book, "The grace of the Lord Jesus be with God's people. Amen." John's vision of God's victory over evil has come to an end. He has written down all he was told to write down. You have it in your hands. You may not understand it all. John didn't understand it all. Who can, after all, understand everything God is doing in your life or in the world? But this should be a comfort to you as it was to those early Christians long ago, "God is in control; He will win; You are not alone; Look at your present life from the perspective of eternity with Him; keep the faith."

STUDY QUESTIONS

Q: If you were advising a Hollywood film producer about making a movie of the book of Revelation, what might you suggest he or she emphasize?

Appendix

COMMENTARIES ON REVELATION

Barclay, W., "The Revelation of St. John" Daily Study Bible, Westminster, 1976

Barnhouse, Donald Grey, "Revelation" Zondervan, 1971

Beasley-Murray, G. R., "Revelation" The New Century Comm., Eerdmans, 1974

Caird, G. B. "The Revelation of Saint John the Divine" A & C Clark,1966

Charles, R. H. "The Revelation of St. John" 2 vols. ICC, T&T Clark, 1920

Ladd, George Eldon, "Revelation" Eerdmans, 1972

Massyngberde-Ford, J. "Revelation" Anchor Bible, Doubleday, 1975

Morris, Leon, The Revelation of St. John" Tyndale NT Comm., Eerdmans, 1969

Mounce, Robert H., "The Book of Revelation" NICNT, Eerdmans, 1977

Thomas, Robert L., "Revelation 1-7" Moody, 1992

Wall, Robert W., "Revelation" Hendrickson, 1991

Walvoord, John F., "The Revelation of Jesus Christ" Moody, 1966

Wilcock, Michael, "The Message of Revelation" IVP, 1975

SUPPLEMENTAL BOOKS ON ESCHATOLOGY

Beasley-Murray, G. R., "Jesus and the Kingdom of God" Eerdmans, 1986

Beasley-Murray, G. R., "Jesus and the Last Days" Hendrickson, 1993

Clouse, Robert G., "The Meaning of the Millennium" IVP, 1977

Gloer, W. Hulitt (Ed.), "Eschatology and the New Testament" Hendrickson, 1988

Ladd, "The Presence of the Future" Eerdmans, 1974

Pentecost, J. Dwight, "Things to Come" Zondervan, 1958

SCRIPTURE REFERENCES

OLD TESTAMENT:

Genesis:
  2:16 (226)
  2:24 (47)
  3:1-5, 14-15 (139)
  3:15 (137-138)
  3:22 (227)

Exodus:
  3:14 (17)

Leviticus:
  26:11-12 (219)

Psalms:
  2:9 (69, 137)
  96:11 (69)
  139:15-16 (18)

Job:
  1:6-12 (141)

Isaiah:
  2:4 (193)
  11:1-2 (15)
  14:12-15 (140)
  22:20-22 (53)
  25:6-9 (193-194)
  53:6-9 (76)
  59:19-21 (98)
  65:15 (193)
  65:17-20 (218)

Jeremiah:
  15:1-2 (155-156)
  31:33 (219)
  51:1-2, 6-7, 12-13, 54-56 (178-179)

Ezekiel:
  1:4-12, 22-28 (61-63)
  2:9-10 (74, 123)
  3:3-4 (123)
  37:26-27 (219)
  39:11-14, 17-20 (195)
Daniel:
  1:3-20 (40-42)
  7:1-8, 11-12, 15-22 (149-151)
  7:9-10 (209)
  7:13 (92, 204)
  7:13-14 (20, 26)
  7:13-22 (156-157)
  9:27 (90)
  10:5-6, 9, 19 (26)
  12:1-3 (143)
Hosea:
  2:16-23 (192)
Joel:
  1:1-7 (117)
  2:1-5, 12-13 (118)
  2:31 (92)
Zechariah:
  3:1-2 (142)
  4:1-5, 11-14 (127-128)
  12:10 (20)

NEW TESTAMENT:
Matthew:
  5:37 (161)
  8:11 (193)
  22:1-14 (197)
  24:1-3 (87)
  24:4-8, 9-14 (88)

18:1-24 (183-185)
19:1-21 (189-191)
20:1-15 (201-203)
21:1-27 (215-217)
22:1-21 (223-225)

OTHER WRITINGS

Aelius Aristides, *Roman Orations*, (186)

II Enoch 29:3-4 (140)

Epistle of Barnabas 15:45 (94)

Nostradamus, *Century 10, Quatrain 72* (92)

Talmud, *Sanhedrin 93b* (16)

Talmud, *Sanhedrin 97a* (93)

Talmud, *Kiddushin* (187)

GLOSSARY

144,000, number of those sealed by God: 91, 100, 101, 103, 116, 159-162

666, mark of the beast: 152-155

Abyss, residence of fallen angles and demons: 115, 119, 128, 140, 215

Aelius Aristides, Greek orator, d. 181 AD: 186

Alexander the Great, King of Macedon, d. 323 BC: 181

Antichrist: 80, 84, 86, 129, 147-148, 154, 161, 172, 175, 177, 181, 194, 196, 210

Antiochus III the Great, d. 187 BC: 50-51

Antiochus IV Epiphanes, son of Antiochus the Great, d. 164 BC: 90, 127

Armageddon: 86, 171, 194

Artemis, Greek goddess in Ephesus: 35, 46

Babylon, Babylonian Captivity: 39-40, 126, 140, 177-178, 180, 183, 185-186

Balaam, prophet of Moab: 45

Barnabas, pseudopigraphical epistle: 93-94

Beasts, first and second: 79, 85, 128-129, 145-149, 151-155, 159-167, 171-177, 180-181, 196

Caligula, Roman Emperor, d. 41 AD:187

Colossae: 14, 56

Appendix

GREEK AND HEBREW WORDS

angelos (Greek) meaning "messenger": 28

ap anatalōn āliou, (Greek) meaning "from the rising of the sun" or "from the East":99

Apocalypse, *apokolupsis* (Greek) meaning "revealing something hidden": 5

diabolos, (Greek) meaning "slanderer, splitter, accuser": 142

ekklesia (Greek) meaning "called-out-ones, church": 13

ethnous, (Greek) meaning "gentiles, nations": 102

Hades (Greek) meaning "Hell, abode of the dead": 27, 210

kairos (Greek) meaning "time, as in the right time": 228

koinonia (Greek) meaning "fellowship": 24

kronos (Greek) meaning "time, as in clock time": 228

krustallo, (Greek) meaning crystal: 65

Martyr, *martus* (Greek) meaning "witness, testifier": 18, 84-85, 109, 121-122, 131, 203, 207

Maranatha, (Aramaic) meaning "Come, O Lord": 109

nai (Greek) meaning "yes, so be it": 21

pantokratōr (Greek) meaning "Almighty": 21

thlipsis, (Greek) meaning "suffering, tribulation": 24, 91

Appendix

Made in the USA
Middletown, DE
18 June 2024

55977560R00146